S·O·U·T·H·E·R·N
AFRICA

CRUCIBLE FOR
CO~OPERATION

s·h·a·r·i·n·g · a · s·u·b·c·o·n·t·i·n·e·n·t

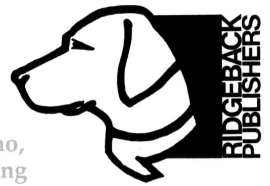

A pragmatic appraisal by top people who, getting about their daily lives, are helping shape the destiny of a subcontinent.

First world achievement and technological know-how sparking the development of a sleeping economic giant – for the good of all the millions who call the subcontinent home.

Ridgeback Publishers

Conceived, Compiled and Edited by

© *DENNIS WINCHESTER~GOULD* 1989

Assisted by LYN HESKETH

Research by JUNE van der MEULEN

ISBN 0-620-13622-7

Reproduction by Industrial Graphics (Pty) Ltd.
Printed and bound by CTP

P·R·O·L·O·G·U·E

MY DREAM – if one may be permitted to dream : the southern half of the continent of Africa, let us give it a name, southern Africa, has all the essentials that will inevitably make it an economic colossus of the future.

Gold, diamonds, platinum, asbestos, uranium, chrome, vanadium, copper – more minerals than any other area of the world can even dream about; mountains, mighty rivers, deserts; rich as nowhere else in its wildlife and birds; more flora species than anywhere else on earth; vast, vast distances snugly embraced by the mighty oceans of the famed Cape sea route; skies forever blue; stars so bright it needs but a hand to reach up and feel them; a motley of peoples, all striving for that quintessential thing – the best kind of living that life can offer; peoples inspired by the technological know-how of their first world component (of whatever race or culture or creed); peoples who, together, will build progressively upon their on-going achievements in fashioning the giant that will uplift them all.

The experiment of the 1950s, the Central African Federation of the Rhodesias and Nyasaland, brought hastily into being by politicians – even more hastily dismembered; well before any significant economic infrastructure could be developed.

Whatever ultimate political shape or form greater southern Africa will take upon itself will be a lasting one; fashioned as it will be by the common interests of its peoples.

A sound economic base is the shaper of politics – politics without economics is but a tool of despots and dictators.

The message for the world is – see, understand, support.

EDITOR

iii

I·N·D·E·X

Personal index — see back

A·R·C·H·I·T·E·C·T·U·R·E

PERCEPTIONS
AND
EVER~CHANGING NEEDS

To meet the challenge of working as Architects in the evolving southern Africa region, to attempt to discover and understand the implications of the work ahead and to develop an individual architectural language and style that is truly of the region, for the region — classically derived and locally evolved — to protect that which is of value in the cultures of all our people for future generations — that is the dream.

GEOF RICHARDSON
Architect

The sun sinks below the African skyline, the stark contrast of modern progress and ancient tradition merge, reducing form and distance to flat silhouette shapes. The myriad pin pricks of electric light compete with the stars for dominance and the city, busy and bustling, slowly settles down for the night.

Close by villagers cook meals over open fires, sharing stories of those gone but not forgotten and oft told legends of long ago.

The dawn brings with it the crisp air, the coo-cooing of the tjorie dove, the ever increasing crescendo of the city-bound traffic and the stark reality of Africa and its struggle to survive the future. A dense cloud of smoke and smog hangs over the shanty areas and a mass of people move into gear to start a working day — a day for some that has a promise of reward and for many others little more than mere survival.

Is Africa destined to remain the dark continent, continuously punishing her people with disease, drought, war and deprivation? Are the lighter tribes to remain elite and separated watching helplessly and with mounting fear as the black nations continue to grow alarmingly, threatening not only them but the people of Africa as a whole? Is there a role to be played by the first world African sector, are there lessons to be learned and can history be reviewed to avoid similar mistakes in the future? Can the first and third world communities merge to form a multi-faceted work and community force that is able to objectively assess and describe the problems, desires, needs and requirements of Africa in the twenty first century?

The African revolution of our time and the liberal minded decolonisation of Africa was fatally shaped by the colonists' weak acceptance of the formula 'one man – one vote – one election – one dictator' and further warped by western contempt for, and disinterest in, the ensuing misfortunes of all Africans (throughout post-colonial Africa).

The southern Africa region is an area where Bushmen roamed, hunted and created superb rock and cave paintings for thousands of years before white and black tribes arrived to appropriate their homelands and co-operate to exterminate them when it was found they could not be tamed.

Laurens van der Post found in these people the earlier stages of man's conscious relationship with the natural processes: the Bushman's intuitive oneness with plant and animal life, evinced, for example, by his ability to find water and navigate a desert featureless to European and even African eyes, and the dreams and myths that animate the Bushman's superb visualisation of nature and man's place in nature, thereby enabling him to live in Africa those many centuries without damaging the ecosystem.

The Bushman's civilised successors, black and white, have taken less than 300 years to erode Africa's natural riches and fertility to a degree that has

now produced (as just a first instalment of outraged nature's revenge) the current famine and flood disasters of the region.

Present day southern Africans have inherited and contributed to a legacy that is fraught with distrust, hatred, racial tension and major socio-economic difficulties. Historically, Black African cultures, particularly their building vernacular, were comprised under the influence of the conquering white tribes, who were themselves facing an architectural capitulation with the advent of the modern movement.

Change and progress must however continue and this needs time, a time-scale different to that of the hurried planning and patching of establishment mentalities – what is needed is a broadening awareness, a recognition of individuals and a careful and considered evaluation of the region as a whole and thereafter reduced down by planning scales to ultimately end up in each man's castle. Africans, like all peoples of the world and even within the misery of poverty and deprivation, have an unconscious wish not to be wanted merely as a cog in an expanded industrial leviathan but wish to feel part of a progression of social development and general improvement in quality of life. There is need to continuously remind the economist – who forever counts cost – that economics makes no sense except in a human context – it will fail if its material instrumentality is not related to classical humanistic preconsiderations – in short

> *''Market economics is a good servant*
> *But a bad master''.*

However uninviting Africa may seem, there is another prospect – that of enormous natural material and labour resources, ideal climatic conditions and opportunities for responsible control and direction of growth, based on a reviewed planning procedure that must take cognisance of the tragic development mistakes of north and south America, Europe, Asia and Africa.

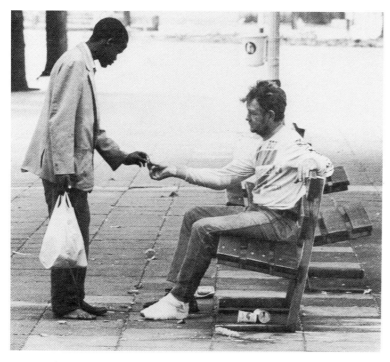

To harness the natural wealth, energy resources, mental and physical strength of the people and to plan within non-prescriptive principles of human consideration and concern can lead to the close co-operation and combined development of the southern Africa region, where countries, states, provinces and governments are subservient to the region's overall development, peace and prosperity.

Planners, statisticians, economists and politicians from the entire region must as a matter of urgency set up organisations to identify existing information available for the southern Africa region, and where this information is lacking, insufficient or unavailable, set out to acquire and correlate whatever is necessary to make long-term accurate and objective projections.

The urbanisation of the southern Africa peoples has been and remains one of the most forbidding problems facing the region. Cumbersome official housing programmes, uncontrolled squatting and fast-expanding populations have resulted in adverse ecological and environmental conditions in the densely populated areas. Any future planning proposals must recognise macro issues and constraints that address the problems of transport, water and energy supply, education, agriculture, political stability and overall philosophies and concepts that are appropriate to socio-economic harmony and human contentment.

A major task awaits all southern Africans in the future − a task which at first appears insurmountable but to the old Bushman talking to Sir Laurens it was simple

"There is a dream dreaming us".

Seen logically or poetically the idea is reassuring − such a principle cannot abandon us for that would be to abandon itself.

Southern Africa, as part of a continent largely unliberated by "political liberation", has, as a stabilising factor, South Africa. Post apartheid times are inevitably close and a period of mutual co-operation and development between all the southern Africa countries hopefully lies ahead. The time is perfect for forgetting and forgiving, for talking and listening − a time when issues of mutual interest and benefit will form the basis of the future for all southern Africans, that we may look to the future with "a song in our hearts and a prayer of praise on our lips".

E·N·E·R·G·Y

POWER TO
A SUBCONTINENT

ENERGY TO LIGHT A SUBCONTINENT

Energy is the key to development, to economic growth and to improve quality of life.

Eskom's product is electricity . . . that most useful and adaptable form of energy. It is not mere coincidence that the development of electrification invariably parallels socio-economic upliftment.

The opening up of the southern African subcontinent into a thriving economic power-house, one of the world's major potential growth areas in the unfolding decades, will depend on the choices we make and the actions we take now.

Radical improvements in economic development in southern Africa require a greater shift towards a developmental approach – not merely a loal focus, but an encompassing, comprehensive regional vision.

I.C. McRAE
Chief Executive
Eskom

The creation of an energy base which utilises the abundant natural resources of southern Africa for the benefit of all its people is not only technically feasible but is an economic necessity. Power technology has no boundaries and as Eskom is the largest power supplier on the continent (60% of all electricity generated in Africa) it is well placed to play a major role in the development of an inter-connected regional grid. Such a grid would make the region interdependent as well as make each of the countries energy independent.

An energy base in each country would mean that the benefits of increased production, incomes and quality of life would accrue to its own people. Based on this common objective Eskom has established many forms of co-operation with governments of neighbour states, and dialogue already exists with utilities and ministers of energy throughout the region.

There is enormous potential for assisting each other: exchanging experience, strategies for industrialisation and technology transfer, and addressing common problems such as electrification of rural areas and urban townships – the latter is a particularly high priority for South Africa where electricity supply to the sophisticated and technologically developed component is generally satisfactory, but supply to the developing sector is either non-existent or insufficient.

As elsewhere on the subcontinent the majority of the population is scattered across rural tribal lands; but increasingly people from these areas are migrating to poor urban townships. Rural electrification must continue to support the development of the rural economy; but an intensified long-term programme of township electrification is now of vital urgency for the rapidly urbanising population. Besides immeasurably improving quality of life, electrification offers opportunities for employment through the development of local and home industries and, via the entry of millions of people into the modern cash economy, supports growth potential.

Time is of course of the essence. Chances for a darkening scenario continue to grow; unless we act quickly our subcontinent will face a bitter struggle to raise itself from poverty. We have to act *NOW*, and act *TOGETHER*, to harness the potential of electrical energy as a major driving force in the industrial and socio-economic development of southern Africa.

To enable us to succeed in achieving our growth potential we need – skills, technology and of course money. Skills development presupposes placing a high priority on education at all levels. Adapting existing first world technology – including technical training – is our second challenge.

First world standards add to the cost of installing electricity, putting it beyond the means of the average family. Electricity must be made available at prices which people can afford, and suppliers of technology must be urged to develop suitable, affordable alternatives. Commitments from governments, local authorities, development aid agencies and foundations are needed to meet requirements by making funds available. A third immediate challenge is to find innovative options for financing electrification schemes, grid expansion and energy resource development – joint ventures, the Black business sector, private supply companies are but three such options.

We need to pool all our resources – before the turn of the century we want to see lights glowing all over, we want to hear the wheels of commerce and industry spinning. We will want to know that the development scenario is alive and well, and still growing!

16

One of the ten largest utilities in the world, Eskom provides electrical energy for . . . . .

. . . . . transport

. . . . . households

. . . . . *mining*
. . . . . *commerce and industry*
. . . . . *agriculture*
. . . . . *harbours*

*Outside the bustling
commercial centres,
millions await electricity.
Eskom engineers have
calculated that, if some of the
stringent requirements are
removed, the cost of
installing electricity
can be halved without
compromising on safety or
security of supply.*

Eskom's objective is to blend its resources with those who have an interest in the realisation of viable solutions for a brighter future . . . . .

. . . . . *improved quality of life*

. . . . . *rural economies*

. . . . . *education and skills*

. . . . . *small business development*

. . . . . *trained people to fulfill a role in a more industrialised society*

20

. . . . . to create a growth scenario of a thriving economic powerhouse that embraces the whole sub-continent

the hardships of alternative energy sources . . . . .

. . . . . . and the devastation caused by deforestation

Vision of the future:. . . . . *power lines, all linked to a huge power grid, striding over national boundaries and spreading out from the Cape to the Equator*

W·A·T·E·R

LIFEBLOOD OF ALL LIFE...
...OF ALL DEVELOPMENT

Surrounding the Witwatersrand is the principal wealth-generating region of the southern Africa subcontinent, but it is a relatively dry part of the globe. Its continued stimulus to the advancement of all the southern Africa states is dependent upon adequate water supplies and the fostering of strong ties of interdependence.

An advanced country such as South Africa can ill afford to have on its doorstep disadvantaged nations, and it is therefore in its interests to initiate steps to rectify the imbalance in wealth generation.

Visionaries were quick to note the stark contrast between the comparatively dry but highly developed south and the well-watered but relatively undeveloped north, and have for long advocated co-operative north-south water and power links as attractive means of stimulating economic take-off among the less developed nations of southern Africa.

DESMOND C. MIDGLEY Pr.Eng.
Emeritus Professor of Hydraulic Engineering (Wits University)
Specialist consultant to WLPU Consulting Engineers.

The southern part of the subcontinent has had its overall water balance frequently subjected to technical scrutiny, and invariably the Vaal-Limpopo system stands out as having an alarmingly steep rise in projected water shortfall. This is clearly attributable to the rapid economic growth rate of the core region which straddles the Vaal-Limpopo divide.

The dominant role of this region is not difficult to explain; it contains the world's greatest storehouse of mineral wealth. Most of the minerals of which production in South Africa ranks first or second in the world, viz. platinum, gold, vanadium, chrome, uranium, iron, manganese, diamonds and fluorspar, come from areas dependent for water upon the Vaal-Limpopo system.

The Vaal-Limpopo area also contains more than two-thirds of the known coal reserves of the whole African continent; these support South Africa's petrochemical complex and the vast coal-fired power station complex which radiates powerlines that feed electricity to the far corners of the subcontinent.

Furthermore, this core region is South Africa's principal granary and seed-oil producing area. It is without doubt the hub of the subcontinent throughout which its influence is strongly felt. But local water resources have long since been exhausted and continued importation is therefore imperative.

The first phase of the Lesotho Highlands scheme is designed to cope with the demand growth of the 1990s. Further tappings of the Upper Orange and escarpment rivers can, at a stretch, meet the projected water demands to about 2020. Long before that time the demands of the core region will have become great enough to warrant development of sources as far away as the Zambezi system. Electrical power is needed for the boosting of water transfer links, so power and water development go hand in hand. The electricity demands of the south will have grown so spectacularly that inter-state links from the south with the enormous potential power sources in the large rivers of Zaire, Angola, Zambia, Malawi and Mocambique will have become not only feasible but also highly attractive.

Pressure will continue to mount to divert water to urban and industrial use. The enormous fund of agricultural know-how and entrepreneurial skills in the south would then expand northwards where vast areas could be developed under irrigation. Suitable soils and water resources abound to meet the needs of starving Africa but technical know-how is required for orderly development. Inter-state co-operation could well achieve this.

If this interdependence is achieved, and there is no valid reason why it should not, living standards will improve, and decentralisation of industrial development will follow.

Water and power are strongly linked; large quantities of water are needed to generate power. Imported power would enable water and coal in the south to be diverted to alternative uses.

The hydro-power resources of central and southern Africa amount to 63% of Africa's total and 17% of the world total, but only the demands of the south warrant large-scale hydro development. The benefits that would flow from extending and densifying the electricity grid throughout the subcontinent are widespread. It is a sobering thought that the energy equivalent of what South Africa's Eskom will be generating in, say, 40 years time — in coal-fired power stations that unavoidably pollute the atmosphere and consume non-renewable resources — has for ages past been dissipating itself in turbulence as the big rivers of the north make their way to the sea.

The revenue to be earned by these energy-exporting states would greatly improve their economies and make them less dependent upon handouts. Their self-esteem would be correspondingly enhanced.

At Inga Falls a hydro station twice the size of the biggest so far in the world would be needed to harness the full potential of the Zaire (Congo) river, but only in the south does there exist the demand for energy generated on that scale. The existing miniature hydro station at Inga, and other somewhat larger installations elsewhere to the north, will for many decades tap only minor proportions of the potential — until the bold decision is taken to negotiate the extension and intensification of the network linking the potential hydro power of the north with the coal-burning stations of the south.

Already Eskom generates more than 60% of the electricity used throughout the African continent, with forward thinking being in terms of nuclear power generation. How much more attractive to develop the pollution-free water power potential of Zaire, Angola, Zambia, Zimbabwe, Malawi and Mocambique in an interconnected subcontinental network!

Co-operation among the
states of southern Africa
in developing their vast
resources could within a
couple of decades raise the
subcontinent to the level
of achievement of the USA
of today — a potential
United States of Southern Africa!

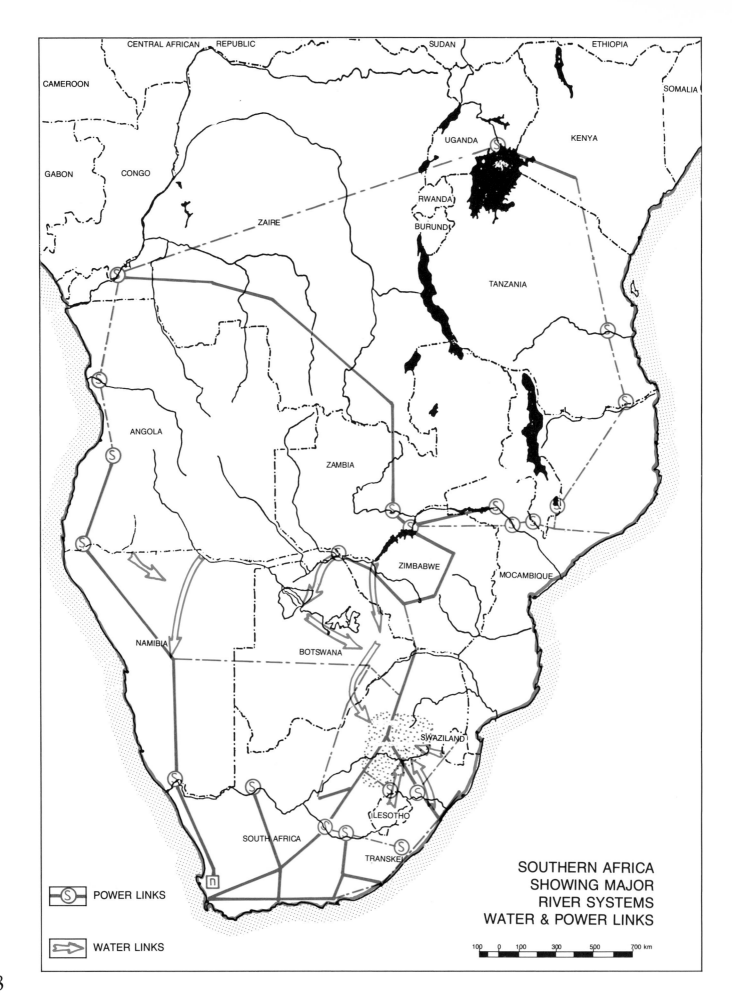

CAMEROON
CENTRAL AFRICAN REPUBLIC
SUDAN
ETHIOPIA
SOMALIA
GABON
CONGO
ZAIRE
UGANDA
KENYA
RWANDA
BURUNDI
TANZANIA
ANGOLA
ZAMBIA
ZIMBABWE
MOCAMBIQUE
NAMIBIA
BOTSWANA
SWAZILAND
SOUTH AFRICA
LESOTHO
TRANSKEI

SOUTHERN AFRICA
SHOWING MAJOR
RIVER SYSTEMS
WATER & POWER LINKS

Ⓢ POWER LINKS

⬡ WATER LINKS

100 0   100   300   500   700 km

28

Southern Africa Water Management
– a co-operative necessity

In all societies water is essential to life, to social development and to economic progress. A major contributor to a higher quality of life in developed societies is the convenient and reliable availability of good quality water.

In semi-arid southern Africa the increasing water demand arising from the growth of the population and the economy has to be met from limited resources that have to be shared between competing

G C D CLAASSENS
Director-General
Department of Water Affairs

user groups and various states. The beneficial joint utilization of the available water depends largely on the extent of co-operation between the various users.

To meet the unfolding situation, the Republic of South Africa (RSA) has developed a resourceful holistic water management strategy which requires the maintenance of a collaborative partnership with all users. As the combined demands of complex partly developed and partly developing societies and economies on the available resources rise, increasing attention is being paid to finding practical compromises to facilitate handling of conflict between legitimate users having widely divergent interests, aspirations and levels of sophistication.

The major goal is to ensure the ongoing, equitable provision of adequate quantities and qualities of water to all competing users according to their particular needs at acceptable degrees of risk and cost under changing conditions. A climate of understanding is being nurtured in which each user group can be induced to accommodate the changing needs and aspirations of others. The water management strategy is also of particular importance in international negotiations concerning the joint utilization of water resources of common interest.

In recent years the DWA has concentrated on interbasin transfers to provide water to drainage areas where economic development is outstripping the natural available resources. Schemes such as the Orange-Fish, Tugela-Vaal, Riviersonderend-Berg River and Komati-Usutu-Vaal Projects are examples of this.

Often the optimal use of water can be achieved only by implementing joint water schemes serving more than one state. The field of international co-operation covers *neighbouring states*, members of the *Economic Community of Southern Africa* (ECOSA), *self-governing territories* and the *Republic of South Africa* (RSA). The broader context includes neighbouring and other states in the subcontinent such as Angola, Mocambique, Namibia, Zambia and Zimbabwe which have the potential to co-operate in the sharing of water and other resources.

A vital issue is that the legitimate aspirations for development of several nations sharing the resources have all to be met equitably. Practical compromises aimed at the best joint utilization by peoples at different levels of development and with different aspirations are being sought for the common good.

Water Commissions have been set up between the RSA and each of its neighbouring states and the ECOSA states to monitor development and to advise the governments concerned on the action required to achieve the best joint utilization of the common water resources. Negotiations on the joint use of water between states have proceeded in accordance with rules drafted in 1966 in Helsinki, Finland, by the International Law Association. The rules embody the principle of equitable sharing which demands that the maximum benefit, with the minimum disadvantage, be provided to each basin state from the use of the common water.

All practical water quality controls, from point-source control to water treatment for removing the deleterious products of eutrophication (or enrichment) of water supplies primarily by nitrates and phosphates, are being considered. Because the number of third world urban concentrations is increasing rapidly, special attention is being given to the development of a low-level phosphate removal technology, commensurate with the level of expertise available for operation of water care works in these areas.

The Hendrik Verwoerd Dam – South Africa's largest dam

The Vaal Dam's water is supplemented from other catchment areas such as the Tugela, Usutu and Slang River basins.

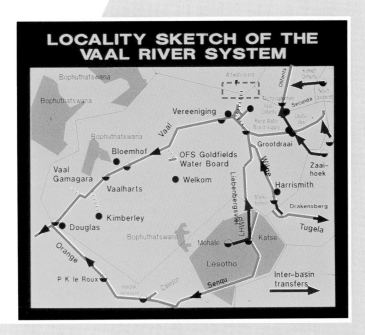

LOCALITY SKETCH OF THE VAAL RIVER SYSTEM

The Vaal River water supply area is the most important supply region in South Africa.

South Africa has always striven to be at the forefront of the state of the art of water engineering. It therefore has much expertise to share with other states. Innovative technology has been introduced for hydrological analyses such as stochastic hydrology and risk analysis, drilling, tunnelling, design, construction of rollcrete dams, water purification, treating and recycling effluent and reducing requirements for power generation.

The progressive outlook also encompasses the development of new water management techniques. A major innovative study is being done into the ideal operation of all facilities serving the Vaal River region, which is the economic heartland of South Africa. It should ensure the optimum management of supply according to principles of quality management and risk analyses to competing user groups with differing demands. Improved planning techniques, including the quantification of the value of intangibles in water allocation, and improved methods of determining phasing and financing are under investigation. Comprehensive basin studies and environmental impact assessments using the latest techniques are also underway.

Some of the latest technology being developed and implemented in South Africa is the use of satellite imagery for quantity and quality management, the use of radar for weather modification and flood forecasting, the use of meteor scatter equipment for data logging from remote sites, and the development of a computerized decision support system and geographic information system. Other trends include increasing attempts to quantify the value of intangible considerations relating to the use of water, such as for maintenance of the ecology and for recreation.

The Orange-Fish Tunnel delivers water from the Orange River to the valley of the Great Fish River and the Sundays River Valley. It is the longest continuous enclosed aqueduct in the southern hemisphere and the second-longest water supply tunnel in the world.

M·I·N·E·R·A·L
T·R·E·A·S·U·R·E·H·O·U·S·E

IN ALL THE WORLD
THERE IS NO RICHER

Besides being the largest employer of mining labour in the western world when oil is excluded, South Africa's 120-year-old mining industry is without question still the most important source of wealth for the diverse nations and peoples of Africa's southern sub-continent and will continue to be so for many decades to come. More than anything else, it reflects the dependence of the region upon South Africa's economy.

COLIN FENTON
President of the Chamber of Mines of South Africa and Deputy-Chairman of Gold Fields of South Africa, Limited

As a non-discriminating, equal opportunity employer paying the same wages for work of the same value, the industry employs some 759 000 people of all races, colours and creeds – about 400 000 more people than the mining industry in the United States, 595 000 more than in Britain, 668 000 more than in Canada and 680 000 more than in Australia.

In terms of the range and importance of the minerals produced, South Africa and its independent homelands are unique. They have more than 40 mineable minerals and account for up to 90 per cent of the free world's production of key minerals – such as vanadium, chrome, manganese and the platinum group metals – vital to the survival of a modern economy.

The discovery of gold over 100 years ago on the Witwatersrand was, above all, instrumental in catapulting South Africa's impoverished, pastoral and largely subsistence economy – aggravated by an arid, hot and hostile hinterland – into the modern and well-developed industrial powerhouse of the subcontinent it is today, the most advanced in the whole of Africa. It not only gave impetus to the development of harbours and the vast network of roads and railways now straddling southern Africa, it spawned many other related and unrelated industries, stimulated the growth of large industrial centres and gave birth to the City of Johannesburg, heart of the largest industrial complex in the southern hemisphere.

Although South Africa only has 10 per cent of Africa's population and occupies only four per cent of the land area, it provides about 60 per cent of the electricity produced on the entire continent, a good barometer of the level of industrial sophistication. Mostly generated from the country's massive coal reserves, almost 30 per cent of power is used by the mining industry.

*Up to 90 per cent of the workers in South
Africa's mines, particularly its labour
intensive gold mines, are unskilled and semi-
skilled, some 60 per cent coming from rural
areas and 40 per cent from the developing areas
of neighbouring Lesotho, Botswana, Malawi,
Mozambique and Swaziland. The earnings of these
540 000 men, which totalled R3,4 billion in 1987,
play a vital role in supporting the regional
and even the national economies of their home
areas and countries, besides improving the
quality of life of their families and
dependants, estimated to number more than
three million.*

About R2 billion of the money earned on South Africa's mines finds its way back to these source communities by way of savings, remittances and consumer goods not readily available back home, besides supplying countries, such as Mozambique and Lesotho, with scarce foreign exchange.

From exploration to final product. Drill cores, chips, bright yellow ammonium chloroplatinate salt, platinum metal sponge and a platinum bar of 99,99% purity.

PLATINUM-
THE METAL OF THE FUTURE

What is platinum?

Platinum is a rare, precious, white metal. It has a density of 21,45 grams per cc which is higher than that of gold. It is a ''noble metal'' which signifies its high resistance to corrosion. In fact, it remains untarnished on heating and retains its lustre to its melting point of 1 769 degrees centigrade. It is a good conductor of electricity and a most effective catalyst.

DON IRELAND
Managing Director
Impala Platinum

All the platinum group (i.e. those metals in the same family, platinum, palladium, rhodium, ruthenium, iridium and osmium) alloy readily with one another and with many other metals, often taking with them their most outstanding characteristic. For instance, a small quantity of iridium or ruthenium added to platinum increases its hardness and strength while rhodium alloyed to platinum increases its brightness. The platinum/palladium/rhodium combination has proved most effective in automobile pollution control while platinum alloyed to rhodium has proved to be the most efficient catalyst for petroleum refining.

What are the major industrial uses of platinum?

Platinum is largely a metal of the 20th century's advanced technology and its uses and applications have grown dramatically.

The automobile industry has become the largest single consumption sector for platinum with the United States leading the way in utilizing platinum-based emissior control technology to combat pollution. The same technology has been adopted in Japan and more recently in Europe, Australia, Korea and Mexico - and it is likely to be expanded further as more countries adopt clean air legislation.

The catalytic qualities of platinum are also essential to the refining of high octane fuels and for the production of nitric acid without which the demand for fertilizer and explosives could not be met. The fuel cell, in which platinum is used as a catalyst to promote the direct conversion of chemical energy into electricity, was first used to provide on-board power in American space craft. Today the United States and Japan are carrying out full scale research programmes into fuel cell applications which have much commercial potential.

Although platinum is the ideal metal for use in the electronics industry, except in certain military and space applications where endurance is of paramount importance, platinum has steadily given way to cheaper metals such as palladium and silver.

Because of its high temperature stability, platinum also continues to be used in the glass and glass-fibre industries and for a wide range of laboratory ware.

In quite a different field, platinum is used in electrodes for pacemakers while platinum compounds are being used effectively in cancer therapy.

Is platinum used in jewellery manufacture?

Platinum is an excellent metal for jewellery. The metal is strong and holds a diamond or other gems securely. It does not cast unwanted light on a diamond or other precious stone. It never tarnishes or needs polishing. Platinum is also ductile and easy to work. And it does not oxidise at working temperatures.

With these properties, it is not surprising that the platinum demand by the jewellery sector, led by Japan, has shown a fairly steady increase and today accounts for 30% of world-wide demand for the metal.

Platinum has become an investment commodity; how does this market operate?

There are several different routes to follow to invest in platinum.

The easiest for the man in the street, is to buy one of the many coins that have been minted in platinum - there are a number of legal tender coins in existence such as the Bophuthatswana Lowe, the Isle of Man's Noble, The People's Republic of China's Panda and many others.

These coins have largely replaced the demand for small bars by the investor. Large bars are less frequently in demand because of the large sums involved. Another avenue of investment has been opened up by the issue of platinum certificates on the Montreal Exchange.

Platinum futures have been traded for many years on the New York Mercantile Exchange and more recently a futures market has been opened in Tokyo. These paper markets, which often trade in over a million ounces a day in futures contracts - compared with a total physical demand of 3 million ounces a year — are highly speculative.

Are supplies of platinum assured for the future?

The platinum market is relatively small - world platinum products is a little more than 3 million ounces, against an estimated 42 million ounces of gold. About 80% of this market is supplied by southern Africa - largely by two producers, Impala Platinum and Rustenburg Platinum. New southern Africa suppliers are entering the market, but most of these operations are relatively small and some time away from commissioning.

In the longer term, southern Africa, led by the two main producers, who both hold proven reserves of platinum group metals, will continue to dominate the supply of platinum worldwide.

Where are the platinum mines in southern Africa situated?

The majority of the platinum mines in southern Africa are situated in Bophuthatswana and in the bushveld complex that stretches across South Africa from Rustenburg to Lydenburg. The Merensky and UG 2 reefs are mined for platinum group metals, while a third reef, the platreef, is under investigation. These areas account for nearly 80% of the world's platinum reserves. A further 15% of world reserves are estimated to be held by Russia.

At the present time some of the world's largest platinum mines are in Bophuthatswana - and platinum provides the largest source of income for that country.

A·R·T B·E·A·U·T·Y

FROM SOME
SOUTHERN AFRICA
CULTURES

ART
ACROSS ALL FRONTIERS

*T*he Goodman Gallery opened in November 1966 and has been dedicated to exhibiting the work of extraordinary contemporary southern African artists together with both famous and avant-garde international artists. We have had many memorable exhibitions, including two one-person shows of Henry Moore and the only major Picasso exhibition ever seen in this country.

Art has no language barriers, nor is it confined to geographic boundaries. It is a proven aesthetic and prophetic messenger to act in an ambassadorial context for every country in the world. Southern Africa with its own particular brand and melange of flavours is no exception.

LINDA GIVON
Managing Director
The Goodman Gallery

It is the continued aim of The Goodman Gallery to encourage the heritage of the nations of southern Africa by the promotion of art, craft and artefacts, especially in the area of beadwork which is amongst the finest in the world. To this end, we are currently helping, both by sponsoring self-help schemes, and by buying the works of the people, thus providing economic growth and spreading the famous cultures internationally. I would like to emphasize that the consideration of preserving and conserving this heritage is our foremost concern, thus we deem it necessary to encourage the growth and expansion of local museum collections before offering the work abroad, so that the culture remains a surviving entity for the future.

The mark of cross-culturation in southern Africa is extremely pertinent, drawing from a melting pot of already established ancient tribal art and translating them into a contemporary idiom. This idiom is the catalyst which has made countries abroad so interested in the socio-political artistic statements of this continent, and has brought fame and recognition to our artists internationally. In the coming years exhibitions and publications abroad are predominant in our programme, particularly in the U.S.A. and Switzerland, thus proving that we are indeed competent in the third world to rank with the first. The vision of extending our language beyond the jungles and borders is now more of a reality than ever.

The more we intermingle culturally, the more we develop and fight the stigma of race barriers and establish a heritage which adds bricks to the temple of our dreams of a major art contribution to all people in this continent.

Norman Catherine
"Untitled II", 1988
Tin can painting
Collection The Artist

Dr Phatuma Seoka
"The Angry Boer"
Painted wood sculpture
Private collection U.S.A.

Two artists whose work we illustrate to illuminate the concept of cross culturation are Norman Catherine, whose paintings are constructed of tin cans, (found objects) which draw on colours and forms of black tradition, although he is white, and Doctor Phatuma Seoka, a rural black artist, who also works with found objects (branches and roots of trees) but draws on white subjects, such as the "Angry Boer". Both reflect the same socio-political environment although they are geographically and socially far apart.

51

Thomas Motswai
"Bus Stop", 1987
Pastel on paper
Private collection

Johannes Segogela from Sekukhuniland has achieved international recognition with his immaculate painted wood sculpture, reflecting both religious and social statements from a distinctly personal use of observation. His work is both humorous and cynical from a rural setting. Tommy Motswai, a young deaf-mute artist from Katlehong township, brings a naive but perceptive overall view of polyglot cultures of southern Africa, depicting wry humour from the urban standpoint. Unknown to each other, they nevertheless share the ambiguous innocence of the people they observe.

Johannes Segogela
"The Meeting", 1988
Carved and painted wood
Collection Schindler Lifts
Basel Switzerland

52

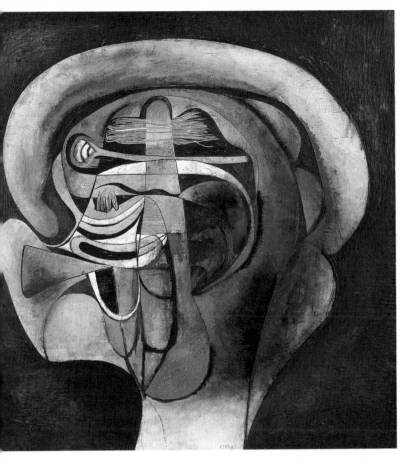

Cecil Skotnes, who has exhibited with our Gallery for 20 years, both in Europe and the U.S.A. as well as in South Africa, has proved his quality as an artist with a universal message, although drawing his inspiration directly from the influence of this continent.

Head III, 1987
Pigments and oils on carved
wood panel 121 x 121 cm
Private collection

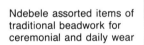

Ndebele assorted items of traditional beadwork for ceremonial and daily wear

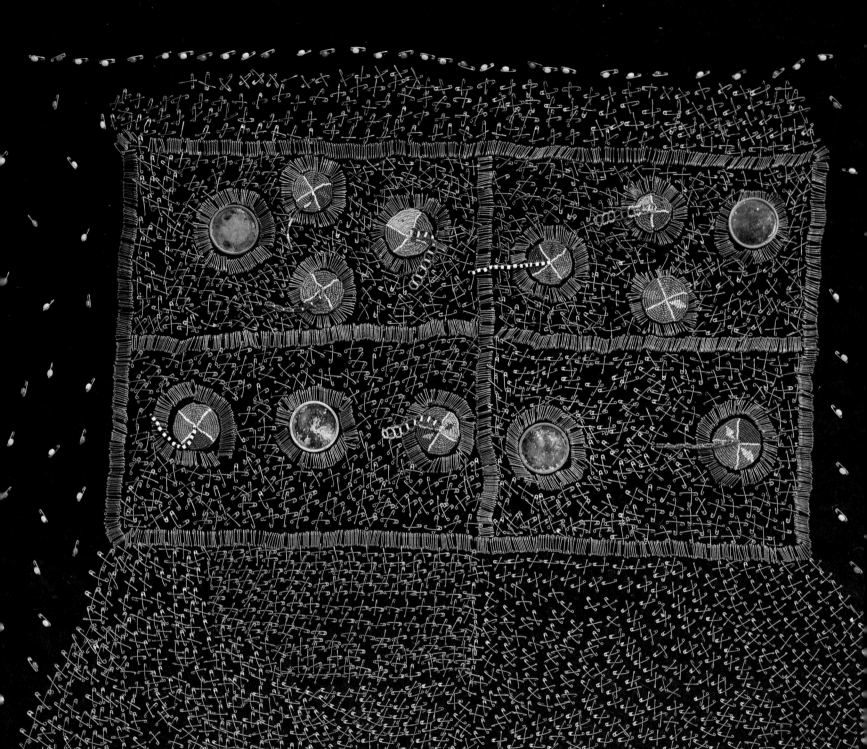

Tsonga:
Ceremonial cloth/
cloak

Collection:
University of
Witwatersrand

Tsonga: Traditional bead basket

Tsonga:
Contemporary
telephone
wire basket

L·I·V·I·N·G B·E·T·T·E·R

MAN'S ETERNAL NEED
AND
WOMAN'S ON-GOING DREAM

In the face of rising unemployment and declining gross domestic products of African countries it is becoming desirable to identify consensus solutions, with the involvement of all the partners, which could achieve targeted goals for development. The next two decades will herald an evolution of the theory and practice of regional co-operation in sub-Sahara Africa.

A.T.N. NELISSEN
Chairman
Premier International

ENGENDERING TRADE BETWEEN NATURAL PARTNERS

The survival of South Africa's role as the economic powerhouse of much of the subcontinent prominently features as a poignant reminder of the potential benefits to be reaped from co-operation rather than from conflict. The natural resources, manpower and infrastructure are here, the market exists, and it should be a spontaneous succession to strive for greater self-sufficiency and trade within the region. Many of the countries are looking for partnerships with sources of technological expertise and investment capital which can be translated into the production of goods and services. What better trading partner exists – a partner that is inextricably tied with Africa, not primarily due to geography but rather by the make-up of the population, by the intricate infrastructural, technological, financial and commercial web that compounds South Africa with the rest of the continent.

It is only if all the parties concerned have a common understanding of the opportunities, potential, concerns and constraints that real progress can be achieved. The necessity to create a climate which will stimulate trade and inter-dependence of the region should also be addressed. The private sector is not only an important participant in engendering regional co-operation – it should play the lead role, and should stimulate definite and practical strategies towards the achievement of these goals. Premier International has already achieved this in many community sectors.

It would be primitive of us to idly stand by and watch while circumstances plot their course. The contribution of the peoples of this region in cultivating momentous growth is to be enhanced, and the nurturing of further progress encouraged, engendering trade between the natural partners.

The next two decades will see the beginning of the theory and practice of regional co-operation in sub-Sahara Africa.

Aspiration engendered through co-operation — a visible future

The private sector should play the lead role in engendering regional co-operation, and should stimulate practical strategies towards the achievement of these goals

The private sector is not only an important participant in engendering regional co-operation – it should play the lead role, as has been done by Premier International who built a stock feed mill in a neighbouring country

The contribution of
the peoples of this region
in cultivating momentous growth
is to be enhanced –
Premier's technicians
tendering education in southern Africa

Wheat

The natural resources, the market exists, for a spontaneous succession of striving for greater self-sufficiency and trade within the subcontinent.

Tea

Coffee

Rail links that compound South Africa with the rest of the subcontinent

Regional co-operation rather than conflict in sub-Sahara Africa

TIMESHARE — SANBONANI

*where unspoilt nature meets
luxurious elegance . . .*

*S*outh Africa is presently one of
the fastest growing timeshare
markets in the world — both in new
resort development and weeks
sold per annum.

Timeshare has created the opportunity for families to enjoy an annual holiday at a reasonable cost. Their investment in timeshare means possessing an ever-appreciating asset in the sense of pegging holiday costs.

A flourishing market exists for timeshare buyers from all over the world, including Europe, America and Australasia, to participate in timeshare. At

HANS HARRI
*Managing Director
Sanbonani*

65

present overseas buyers can acquire local timeshare on a discount against their own countries' opportunities. A further incentive — 50% in financial rand and 50% in commercial rand gives an added discount of approximately 20%. As most of the sought-after resorts in South Africa are linked to RCI for exchange, the door is wide open to overseas buyers to purchase timeshare at plus/minus half the price payable for top resorts in their own countries — and with equal or better accommodation. Many resorts are run on the lines of five-star hotels — and how many countries can compete with southern Africa's natural beauty which takes in deserts, and mountains, and abundant wildlife and fabulous coastal resorts in addition to rich and variable vegetation?

> *Our strong first world component has the potential to lead the way for the rest of southern Africa. Timeshare has to be the answer for the family to combat spiralling hotel and resort costs, and to making southern Africa's places of incomparable beauty available to everyone.*

''Sanbonani,'' my new timeshare resort, commenced in the beginning of 1988. Sanbonani is situated in the eastern Transvaal Lowveld where the Sabie and North Sand rivers meet. The resort blends in with unspoilt wilderness, and preserves the fine ecological balance between man and nature. Age-old giant fig and marula trees provide food for a huge variety of birds and animals which have their home in this paradise between the rivers.

A private nature reserve for timeshare owners lies across the river with a hiking trail through unspoilt bush, alive with animals and birds, to the top of the mountain range. Hippos are permanent residents, and at night graze in the grounds of the resort.

Sanbonani is located within easy reach of the world-renowned Kruger National Park, and many other scenic attractions such as Pilgrims Rest, God's Window, and the Blyde River Canyon — to name but a few.

Sanbonani's facilities are of the highest standard. The complex will comprise one hundred units — thirty units were completed by January 1989. A central complex, presently under construction, with hot water mineral and cold water swimming pools, bowls, tennis, putt-putt, squash and other facilities, will be completed before the end of 1989.

Sanbonani is linked to a hunting/game farm a little over an hour's drive away. Guests wishing to hunt are taken out by arrangement by professional hunters, while for non-hunters a weekend amid the big game could round off the week's stay.

When buying timeshare what has one to look out for? First time buyers should be sure they know what they want, and then not let themselves get talked into buying by sales agencies. Make sure too that the resort is affiliated to RCI, so that you can opt for exchanges with other resorts either locally or overseas.

Nature lovers from all over the world can enjoy this paradise of wilderness and wildlife — and still have the luxurious facilities of Sanbonani.

Take a stroll beside the water and over the bridge surrounded by indigenous shrubs and trees.

*Our strong first world component has the potential to
show the way for the rest of southern Africa. Timeshare
is the family's answer to spiralling hotel and resort costs.*

*Bedrooms are tastefully furnished
with modern furniture all blending
in with African themes.
Bathrooms sport the most modern fittings*

An ever-increasing stream of timeshare tourists and hunters will play a vital role in helping preserve this wonderful bastion of nature's bounty.

Timeshare hunting, under professional supervision, is one of Sanbonani's highlights – or if you don't want to shoot just walk and enjoy the wildlife.

Sanbonani setting off the beauty of an African sunset

H·E·A·L·T·H

VITAL FOR
MAN AND ANIMAL

I. R. TRYTHALL
Head: Pharmaceutical Division
Sandoz Products

73

A FUTURE for MEDICAL and PHARMACEUTICAL SCIENCES In SOUTHERN AFRICA

South Africa, ranked as the world's 24th largest economy outside the CMEA in 1985, increasingly recognises the need to develop further its economic and social ties with its fellow southern Africa states. Industrial interdependence between these states already exists through: transport, energy, agriculture, and mining. However, these industries are largely based on resources and either low and/or known technologies. The breadth of higher scientific and medical expertise, education and technology, which is available here, is however missing elsewhere in the African subcontinent. So, although the neighbouring states provide good primary health care, patients requiring treatments of more complex diseases come here.

There is therefore a real need to stimulate and encourage these neighbouring states to expand their medical facilities and expertise, through closer links with each other and ourselves. By developing and exchanging medical education and research, the countries of southern Africa could improve their relationships and ultimately their future prosperity.

The most effective immunosuppressant is one recently discovered by Sandoz. Its use — to date it has been given to more than 10 000 kidney transplant recipients — has significantly improved graft survival rates. The number of transplant operations being performed has also increased — because the chances of success are better! Eight of the highest distinctions that a drug can win have been awarded to Sandoz for this compound.

PHOTOGRAPH OPPOSITE PAGE
Kidney transplant patients.
Brother gave a kidney to his sister

The practice, the development and the raising of medical standards are dependent on education levels. In the region we have the capability and capacity to finance extensively education. So, it is expected that our neighbours may increase their dependency not only industrially, but more importantly for the region, also educationally. For development in this new-found responsibility and role we need to recognise quickly that we must develop from an economy based primarily on natural resources and manufacturing industries, to one that embraces much more broadly science and technology, and then we must actively institute policies which encourage more research and development.

In strategic terms we must build on our strengths, and in our medical research institutions there are considerable strengths and resources. Indeed, it may well be one of those strengths that has been little recognised, and underexploited.

South Africa, as the medical powerhouse of the southern Africa region, has seven medical schools from which approximately 1 000 doctors graduate annually. An increasingly larger proportion of these graduates are Indians and Africans, who are desperately needed for the future of health care in southern Africa.

Not only have we high medical education standards, but we also have excellent research facilities, in which to conduct medical and pharmaceutical research. We have the capability to provide trained researchers and technologists, who are essential to the advancement of the medical and pharmaceutical sciences. We have over the past several decades developed a sound infrastructure, part of which includes a number of major medical centres which enjoy worldwide fame. Indeed, many individual researchers of worldwide recognition conduct their work here.

MEDUNSA
Medical University of South Africa

1 800 students
— many from Swaziland
  Lesotho, Zimbabwe,
  Namibia and Malawi.

180 postgraduates
— Whites, Blacks,
  Indians and Coloureds.

180 graduates in 1988

In few other countries can there be found the demographics and the diversity, under such a sophisticated medical and health care system, which provides the opportunity for researching so many different and unique conditions. In terms of clinical research, we have excellent possibilities to research innovative and exciting drugs in a variety of race groups under well controlled conditions. Knowledge gained under such circumstances may be of enormous benefit to other multi-racial societies, because it is well established that not all people and races respond to drug theraphy homogeneously. We also have the facilities to investigate, to high international standards, new treatments for the devastating diseases which plague the tropical and third world countries of the globe. And lastly southern Africa has excellent animal and primate colonies which could be part of a more extensive toxicological and pharmacological research programme, whose findings could then be of interest and use to international health and drug regulatory authorities.

There are perhaps two distinct worldwide trends which could be exploited locally if we are determined enough to pursue a future course of increased medical research and education.

Firstly, there is the recognition by the medical teaching centres around the world of the ever growing symbiotic relationship between themselves and the pharmaceutical industry. Here virtually all the multi-national pharmaceutical companies are represented and compete with several major domestically based companies, which export to the other southern African states and throughout the world. In fact, South Africa is the home base of the largest pharmaceutical manufacturer in the southern hemisphere. Many of these companies conduct research and development of significant domestic and international importance in close association with the medical schools and other research institutions within the country.

No longer are new drug discoveries being developed solely in the total isolation of the centralised laboratories of these large enterprises, but rather in closer collaboration with leading medical research centres around the world. This is a significant development, as these centres act as essential and independent validators of research. The industry draws upon this knowledge as an integral part of its research and development programmes. We could increase our participation in the process.

Secondly, there is the emerging shift towards the biotechnologies as a source of new drug entities, away from the highly centralised and high costs of chemical based pharmaceutical research. Biotechnologies have the advantage that they can be researched on a small scale initially, in a good university setting. Whenever a significant advance emerges the pharmaceutical industry can be called upon to support further testing, development and ultimately marketing and distribution of the emergent drug on a worldwide basis.

Like Canada (for example), ours is essentially a resource and manufacture based economy. In more recent times, Canada has certainly recognised the need to encourage the shift towards higher technologies and sees medical and pharmaceutical sciences as among its future economic bases. We should consider seriously to develop our current strength of internationally recognised medical and pharmaceutical research by investing further to encourage more research in collaboration with our medical institutes and the pharmaceutical industry. Why? Because firstly, we already have the high medical standards; secondly, highly reputable universities and medical schools and, thirdly, the significant presence of the pharmaceutical industry, which wishes to work more closely with these medical schools.

In this way we could contribute significantly to the raising of health care standards, and medical education levels throughout the southern Africa region, and perhaps one day become a leader in the development of treatments for tropical and third world diseases.

Pilot Plant Operation, part of a R6,5-million research and development facility in Port Elizabeth. (Lennon)

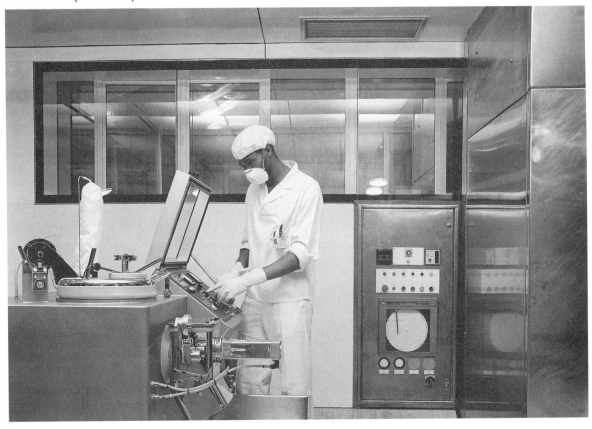

ONDERSTEPOORT

world recognised Veterinary Research Institute

Fighting animal diseases in southern Africa

*A starving continent, Africa
should regard the production of food
as one of its top priorities.*

DR. D.W. VERWOERD
Director
Veterinary Research Institute
Onderstepoort

A major factor affecting food production is animal disease, and the seriousness of this factor in developing countries is brought out in the Food and Agriculture Organisation's statistics which indicate that 75% of the world's population and 60%-70% of the world's livestock are found in these developing countries while only 30% of the total meat is produced there.

Many of the third world countries are in the tropical and sub-tropical regions, and diseases that are unknown in temperate climates abound in these areas and play havoc with the health performance of both man and animal. Research into the nature of these diseases, and the development of measures to control them, are of the utmost importance for survival on our continent.

Nagana or sleeping sickness, East Coast fever, or theileriosis, rinderpest, lung sickness and foot-and-mouth are among the diseases which affect cattle. These diseases do not recognise national borders and all too often these borders in Africa are man-made, without natural barriers such as mountain ranges, rivers or oceans, to make them effective.

The abundance of wildlife, including the ticks and insects which transmit these diseases, show little respect for fences or lines drawn on paper. This makes disease problems truly international in Africa, and no country can deal effectively with them on its own. Even though South Africa has managed to eradicate a few diseases they remain a constant threat from outside our borders. It is thus in the best interests of all concerned to collaborate as closely as possible to control the spread of disease and, wherever possible, eradicate it completely.

South Africa is in a favourable position to assist its neighbours. With more than ten times as many veterinarians as any of the other countries in southern Africa it has well organised veterinary services experienced in the control and eradication of stock diseases and supported by regional diagnostic laboratories. Its veterinary expertise is soundly based on research results generated by the national Veterinary Research Institute at Onderstepoort and the two faculties of Veterinary Science at the universities of Pretoria and Medunsa. These faculties train veterinary students of all race groups.

Onderstepoort is the major manufacturer of livestock vaccines in southern Africa. No less than 72 different biological products are produced, and the annual sales amount to around 160 million doses. It is estimated that about

20% of this production finds its way to neighbouring countries. Many of these vaccines developed at Onderstepoort are not available from any other source.

Private companies play an important role in the provision of stock remedies. In addition to distributing Onderstepoort's vaccines vaccines for pet animals and the poultry industry are imported and pharmaceutical products for the treatment of disease and parasitic infestations are tested under African conditions before being marketed.

Scientists at Onderstepoort are constantly engaged in research on the many diseases still threatening our livestock. The ultimate aim is to develop better diagnostic techniques, and new or improved control measures. Over the years considerable expertise has accumulated in these fields, and this expertise is freely available to any country in our subcontinent.

The past decade has seen a growing awareness of our interdependence as far as the struggle against animal disease is concerned. This is reflected in growing numbers of African scientists visiting Onderstepoort, invitations to our scientists to visit neighbouring countries, increasing correspondence and requests for technical information, and no less than 12 000 specimens submitted for diagnostic purposes during the past 2 years.

One of the biggest crises facing Africa is the starvation of its rapidly increasing population. Control of animal diseases will be one of the most important solutions to this problem and South Africa, with its wealth of expertise and experience, can and will play an increasingly important role in solving the unique problems of this continent.

Much has been accomplished already,
but much more remains to be done.

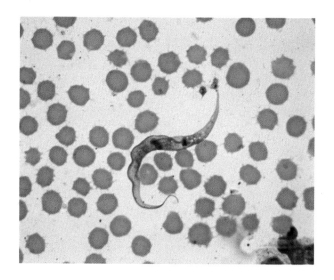

A trypanosoma parasite, which is the causal agent of nagana in cattle, lying amongst red blood cells

The single most important disease in Africa affecting cattle, other livestock and man, is nagana, or sleeping sickness, caused by a blood parasite called *Trypanosoma* and transmitted by the tsetse fly. Large areas of South Africa were unsuited for cattle farming until the tsetse fly was eradicated during the early forties of this century, and a constant threat exists today of the disease crossing the border from Mocambique, where 80% of the surface area is still infested with tsetse flies and cattle farming is thus perforce limited to the remaining 20%.

Roughly one-third of Africa is covered by the so-called 'fly-belt' and it is estimated that the total cattle population of the continent could, at the least, be doubled if the tsetse fly were eradicated completely.

The tsetse fly, which is responsible for transmitting nagana and other diseases caused by trypanosomes

East Coast fever, or theileriosis, is the second big economic scourge of Africa. It is the main constraint on cattle production in east and central Africa, and is caused by a blood parasite transmitted by ticks. The disease has been eradicated from South Africa by a dipping programme of all cattle, strictly enforced by its veterinary authorities, but it took 50 years, and over R100 million, to accomplish this.

Still endemic in countries such as Mocambique, Malawi and Zambia a re-introduction into South Africa remains a constant threat.

A variety of tick species occur in southern Africa and are responsible for the transmission of a number of hemoparasitic animal diseases, of which East Coast fever is one of the most important

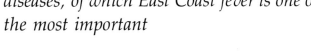

Dipping of cattle to combat tick infestation

86

Three highly infectious diseases, transmitted by contact, which affect cattle are rinderpest, lung sickness and foot-and-mouth. These diseases have been brought under control by the development of vaccines, and well organised vaccination campaigns.

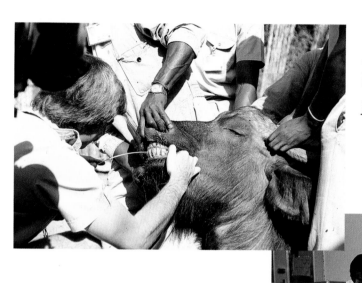

Specimens are taken from a buffalo calf for the diagnosis of foot-and-mouth disease

Serological tests being carried out in the laboratory on specimens submitted for diagnosis

Foot-and-mouth disease, which is carried by many wild animals such as the African buffalo, poses a threat from Mocambique. World-renowned Kruger National Park, allowing free access to buffalo from Mocambique, has to be regarded as an endemic area, and has necessitated the Park having to be fenced on the South African side. If the disease were to spread beyond this area it could have serious economic consequences, as the total export trade in animal products, amounting to at least R1 000 million, would be jeopardised.

A rinderpest epidemic which swept through Africa at the turn of the century killed off 50% of South Africa's cattle herd, as well as large numbers of wild animals. It has been eradicated from southern Africa but

The manufacture of vaccines constitutes one of the major activities of the Veterinary Research Institute, complementing its research programmes and diagnostic services

remains endemic in west and central Africa, and during recent years has flared up again in those countries and is slowly spreading southwards. The World Bank, inter alia, recently launched a campaign to attempt eradication, but the susceptibility of the African buffalo and several antelope species poses a difficult logistic problem.

Lung sickness has also been eradicated from South Africa but remains prevalent in western African countries from Angola northwards.

T·R·O·P·H·Y H·U·N·T·I·N·G

HELPING PRESERVE
WILDLIFE

Trophy Hunting *– preserving our wildlife*

When people, especially those in the northern regions of our world, think of Africa they conjure up a kaleidoscope of images of unique peoples, and of a raw, stark, savage ancient and untamed land – but mostly they think about Africa's wildlife, unequalled, unrivalled anywhere else in the world.

Early writings on Africa gave a picture of seeming endless herds of antelope, and those that fed on them, propagating themselves endlessly and maintaining the status quo. This idyllic dream is unfortunately far from reality. As man's need for space and food increases so does the threat to game animals and to their habitat. More and more cattle and sheep run now where once wild animals flourished, with debilitating effect upon the land; so much so that soil erosion and eventual desertification become inevitable.

TREVOR SHAW
Owner
Zulu Nyala Game Reserve

Poaching has reached crisis proportions in some areas, where local populations regard wild animals as a source of protein. Rhinos, especially the black species, are being rapidly decimated for their horns. In some areas they have already disappeared. In northern Zimbabwe a new bush war has flared up – armed poachers, using AK47 rifles, are crossing the Zambezi from Zambia to kill off the remaining few black rhinos. Zimbabwe Parks Board officials are doing their best to defend the rhino, sometimes forfeiting their lives in the process.

I paint a rather bleak picture, showing a trend which if left unchecked will surely mean the end of wildlife as we know it. Thank goodness, though, it is in the nature of man, when he encounters a problem, to do his best to overcome it; and hopefully in time these destructive practices will, through education, be halted, and a viable game population will be restored.

For game to survive on a long-term basis it needs two essentials viz. protection and economic viability.

There are, in southern Africa, more and more areas of land being set aside for the purpose of protecting wildlife. The famous Kruger, Etosha and Natal Parks, to say nothing of Wankie, and Luangwa Valley, and Kafue, and other state-owned sanctuaries are priceless havens, but their sizes, with few exceptions, cannot be increased. If wildlife populations are to be not only maintained but increased more land must be made available, and this brings me to economic viability.

For wildlife to ensure their continued existence they must, economically speaking, stand on their own four feet. This is where privately owned and managed game reserves come in – more and more are being established, and developed.

Why this sudden renaissance and renewed interest?

The quick answer is tourism and trophy hunting. Many tourists will tell you the principal reason for their visiting southern Africa is to see wild animals.

These areas are becoming increasingly available to trophy hunters/sportsmen, who selectively take only old male animals for their horn size – this does not reduce the breeding potential.

I have owned and managed Zulu Nyala Safaris for the past 8 years, and am more than pleased with the results I have achieved. 99% of the foreign hunters who come to my game reserve in Zululand are totally ethical – true sportsmen and sportswomen. They are, in the truest sense, conservationists. In some instances paying hunters are the only source of income for game ranchers. Naturally, as hunters increase in number so will more and more land and game need to be provided. As only 2%-3% of the animals qualify as trophy animals it is axiomatic that hunters not only do not decrease game populations but are actively responsible for boosting them. Hunters pay in foreign currency, and on average spend 12 times more than the average tourist.

C·O·M·M·U·N·I·C·A·T·I·N·G

UNDERSTANDING

COMMUNICATION IN SOUTHERN AFRICA

The very diverse and pluralistic nature of our society makes communication a major problem both in an industrial/commercial context and in mass communication terms. The population structure of our society is such that communication has to take place not only in a wide variety of languages but it also needs to be structured in order to be understood.

D J KELLY
Managing Director
Bates Wells – Group Services

95

MASS MEDIA COMMUNICATION

Southern Africa's interesting blend of first and third world societies is reflected in the mass media. As with most developing societies broadcast media are playing an increasingly important role. In the countries constituting ECOSA (Economic Community of Southern Africa) there are some 14 commercial TV channels mostly state controlled, although some are privately owned and there is one subscription service which is private. These stations broadcast in 15 different languages and dialects. Programming is a mix of local and imported popular entertainment.

In addition to TV services there are some 80 radio stations in the region broadcasting news, music and entertainment in more than twenty dialects catering to more localised and sometimes less sophisticated needs.

Due to the region's comparatively late entry into television (South Africa 1976, Swaziland 1977) the local stations were able to capitalise on the huge technical advances that had been made internationally. As such the industry is surprisingly well abreast of modern technology with a sophisticated infrastructure and technical quality of the highest order. Opportunities for the further development of new channels (subscription possibly) exist and the viability of using television and radio for education – particularly in rural areas – is being widely explored. Further development of radio is being pursued and in many cases the physical infrastructure and broadcast capacity for these projects exist.

Print media in ECOSA are robust and diverse. Due to the relatively late arrival of TV in the region, print media remained buoyant longer than their third world counterparts, and in large part the industry kept pace with world standards. Almost all publishers are privately and not state held, and reasonable – sometimes surprising – press freedom exists. National, regional and local newspapers abound as do magazines ranging from serious business to consumer publications. Publishing is mainly in English although there are publications of substance in at least 15 other languages.

IN-COMPANY

Given the diverse nature of the region's population – not only linguistically but culturally as well – in-company communication has an area of difficulty often giving rise to conflict, particularly in recent years since the widespread establishment of trade unions.

Commerce and industry in South Africa have spent significant sums of money researching communications methodologies, and interesting and effective techniques have been developed for improving in-company communication.

The application of these systems and techniques is creating a far more constructive and therefore productive working environment in the region. Understanding and use of these concepts is also enhancing training in the workplace.

Southern Africa's communication needs are complex and diverse but the region is uniquely equipped to deal with these problems and in many cases lead development work.

Given the environment in which communication takes place and the added interference factors in a multi-cultural society these strategies are of increased importance.

T·R·A·N·S·P·O·R·T·I·N·G

PEOPLE AND GOODS

TRANSPORTING
– a subcontinent on the move

ROMAN W. SZYMONOWICZ
Managing Director
Associated Automotive Distributors

While archaeologists learn about ancient cities from their buildings and libraries, perhaps future scholars will analyse southern Africa from its transport system.

Both conventional and informal transport methods extend across this vast land mass with its variable climate and uncompromising terrain. Its past is a tribute to man the pathfinder, rolling back the frontiers – pushing on to unconquered ground. Nor is there any sign of a halt to such pioneering. Growth in the subcontinent is such that mass transport systems struggle to cope.

The infrastructural costs of roads and railways are prohibitive across such unyielding landscapes. Moreover, history has shown that such fixed transport methods are efficient only for moving bulk over long distances. Temperatures range from well below zero in some areas to freak sizzling heat in others. There are extremes according to time of year or time of day. Arid areas unspattered by raindrops to belts of intense humidity.

It is in this world that Associated Automotive Distributors took root. Since Land Rovers replaced camels as the only means of transport that could cope with the Kalahari, the company has been advancing with the people into every unexpected corner of the land.

Providing buses to carry people from home to school to work or place of leisure. Trucks to move eagerly-awaited goods. Land Rovers to cross desert or beach or mountain pass – where no other vehicles can travel. Plus the service and parts support that keep these tough vehicles on the road.

Available at all strategic points. Providing jobs and career opportunities at all levels.

Serving every branch of the community. Industry and mining. Farming and forestry. Emergency services such as firefighting. Leisure. Outside broadcast vans to take crews to inaccessible spots.

This is the role of AAD. Helping people throughout southern Africa stay in touch.

Through understanding the character of the landscape and the demands it makes on vehicles. Throughout recognising that managing a transport company in this environment calls for vastly different skills. Through sharing a vision that as long as people and goods need to get from one place to another AAD will be part of this tableau.

Taking foreign visitors close to the action at the exclusive MalaMala Game Reserve

Buses to carry people to school, work or place of leisure

106

Avis Rent A Car

To travel hopefully is better than to arrive, Robert Louis Stevenson once wrote, and no doubt that was true in the spacious and leisurely days of the late nineteenth century. In our own more pressurised times, however, the prospective voyager requires the sure and certain knowledge that the arrival as well as the trip will be handled with impeccable efficiency. The modern traveller, whether corporate executive or tourist, expects a well-developed transport infrastructure even – perhaps especially – when he ventures into undeveloped areas.

It is now more than 40 years since Warren E Avis started the world's first car rental service for air travellers at an airport near Detroit. Since then, car rental has developed into an indispensable link in the business and leisure travel chain. As the major carriers and their feeder airlines have reached out further and further, into the remotest corners of the world, so the car rental industry has kept pace, constantly expanding to provide the air traveller with ground transport when he steps off the plane.

This has also been the case in southern Africa. From its regional base in South Africa, Avis's subcontinent network has reached out to cover Botswana, Lesotho, Malawi, Namibia, Swaziland and Zimbabwe with more than 100 branches. In each case, it has set up an indigenous operation with a local part-

TONY LANGLEY
Managing Director

Avis Rent A Car has established what is believed to be the South African travel industry's technologically most advanced reservations centre at its Isando headquarters

Mr Tony Langley inspects one of cars on the Avis fleet

ner as well as local employees, and equipped it with the facilities, systems and, perhaps most important, the training to function as a fully fledged member of the Avis family.

As such, each of these regional operations is linked directly to Avis's world-wide reservations systems, making it possible, for example, for a businessman in Frankfurt to book a car in Swakopmund with a single phone call to his local Avis branch. Similarly, a Zimbabwean can reserve a car at Heathrow airport by calling Avis in Harare.

The convenience of a car rental network which comprehensively covers the sub-continent, combined with the facility of an international reservations system, has important implications for trade and tourism. So too has the confidence inspired in the intending visitor by the knowledge that, wherever he travels in southern Africa, he can count on the worldwide consistency of product and service guaranteed by the Avis name. For its part, Avis actively promotes these countries with their unique tourist attractions – among them, the Namib desert, Victoria Falls, Lake Malawi and the Botswana nature reserves – in its international marketing campaigns.

From its regional base in South Africa, Avis has reached out to co Botswana, Lesotho, Malawi, Namibia, Swaziland and Zimbabw

The system works both ways, of course. It equally serves, and is as convenient for, the local businessman or holidaymaker who wishes to travel abroad and has domestic access to Avis. Not only can he reserve a car at virtually any airline-served destination in the world, he can pay for it back home in his own currency.

It is my personal belief that as a rule there are more factors which unite people than divide them, even in a region as notorious for its conflicts and contrasts as southern Africa. Trade is one of those things which tend to transcend boundaries and beliefs, and travel, they say, has the wonderful effect of broadening the mind. The expansion of southern African travel and trade will bring greater prosperity to a continent which desperately needs it. In the long run, and this is perhaps even more important, it could also encourage external understanding and internal co-operation.

108

macs maritime carrier shipping

*A*s a shipping line, with ships sailing to and from southern African ports and those in Europe, we carry merchandise (known as ''cargoes'' in shipping terms) of all descriptions, which is loaded in one port and discharged at another. The cargoes are moved from their points of origin to the load port, and from their discharge port to the point of final destination, by means of road, or rail trucks, or barges.

LUCAS de ROMIJN
Managing Director

MAIN PICTURE: *Macs owned specially modified multi-purpose cargo ship*
INSET TOP RIGHT: *Ship's cranes capable of lifting 25 ton pieces*
INSET BOTTOM LEFT: *Combined harvesters – ships are capable of carrying heavy machinery*

Shippers (exporters) utilise the services of a forwarding agent (or their own shipping department) to arrange transport and documentation up to the load port, while receivers (importers) utilise clearing agents on their side.

Ports therefore play a very important role in the despatch and receipt of cargoes, and by thus facilitating trade between one country and another not only develop trade but break down social and economic barriers as well. In the future, the growth and prosperity of the southern Africa subcontinent will depend extensively on South African ports and the ships that serve them.

South African ports are well equipped, with an infrastructure that enables them to handle the full spectrum of cargoes – containerised, break-bulk (e.g. copper, tin, zinc and foodstuffs) and bulk (e.g. fertilisers, ores and minerals). They also handle heavy lifts of machinery, so essential for the infrastructural development of the whole of southern Africa.

In a very real sense South African
ports must be regarded as the gateway
for the development of the entire region.

A valid comparison can be drawn between our ports and the legendary ports of Europe, such as Hamburg, Rotterdam, Antwerp, Zeebrugge and Le Havre. These ports all serve a vast hinterland, and not just the countries in which they are located. Thus they provide a service to the entire common market, as well as to many east-bloc countries, and Scandinavia. This despite the fact that nearly all these countries have their own ports. The message is clear – despite political and social differences economics will dominate.

The situation will be similar here. Populations will grow, and as inter-state trading is stimulated buying power will increase. The vital terminals, or ports, will be called upon to keep pace, and will have to modify their infrastructures to enable them to cope with an ever-increasing range and volume of cargoes.

Naturally this will increase competition between ports, leading to quicker and less expensive handling, greater efficiency, and generally better service.

As South Africa's ports develop, ports in other maritime southern Africa countries will have to do likewise, and this will contribute to the general economic well-being of all the countries comprising the sub-continent.

I believe sincerely this is not just wishful thinking, or a pipe-dream. Shipping, as well as the ports served, are vital for the development of a potentially viable sub-continent – for the benefit of everyone who lives in it.

MINING
MACHINERY
DESTINED
FOR
BOTSWANA

sOUTHAFRICANTRANSPORTSERVICES

An inspiration to its third world neighbours

A reality of life is that transport and trade are inseparable partners in the well-being of any country – in this instance a group of countries, namely southern Africa. Together they form an integrated economic system in which the balance of forces have to be carefully managed to ensure that everybody can benefit.

Such a system is sensitive to the advantage maritime countries have over landlocked neighbours, and to bad performance standards in any of the parts of the transport system. South African Transport Services (SATS) sets an example for all. Its harbours are not used to exploit its landlocked neighbours economically. Furthermore, its railway system, the best developed on the subcontinent, guarantees speedy deliveries of both exported and imported goods. It is for this reason our

BARRY LESSING
Chief Executive –
South African Railways

neighbours attach more value to the quality of our service than to the fact that their goods have to travel a longer distance over South African routes. Because road systems are largely underdeveloped there is a great reliance on railways.

Recent studies undertaken by independent overseas researchers indicate that in 1985 the nine major railway operating countries had a total population of 68 million. South Africa's population then was 32 million, making a total of 100 million in the region.

An interesting fact that emerged is that South Africa accounted for 75% of the region's GDP and two-thirds of its exports. Provides almost 50% of the imports of our landlocked neighbours, and also takes 13% of their visible exports.

Cape Town harbour.

Cargo handled during 1987/88 approximately 5 million tonnes

Number of vessels calling at South African harbours during 1987/88 was 12 725. Total cargo handled during the same period – 94,5 million tonnes.

Centralised traffic control centre. Automatic through-routing of trains is provided together with train-time printing and train-graph plotting

During the past financial year our railways have handled more than 3,6 million tonnes of goods for our neighbours. As part of the various business arrangements there are on average 8 000 units of rolling stock on the lines of other railways in southern Africa at any one time, representing a replacement value of some R700 million. SATS also leases locomotives, aircraft equipment and parts to our trading partners, and provides technical advice and help covering maintenance of all modes of transport systems and infrastructure.

IRON ORE TRAIN

en route for Saldanha Bay harbour

Iron ore exported during 1987/88 was 8 million tonnes

Goods — *the number of revenue-earning goods vehicles is 151 972. Their carrying capacity amounts to 6 5 million tonnes — average of 44 05 tonnes per truck*

SATS is recognised as among the world leaders in various fields of transportation such as containerisation and harbour terminal performance. Because of this many of our trading partners make full use of the outstanding training facilities available to them in the various fields in which we are active.

One does not create permanent prosperity by giving gifts. SATS tries to be enabling — by ensuring that co-operation with the railways in our neighbouring states is governed by business principles. All services and assistance are paid for, and to ensure this we have business agreements with most of the railways in southern Africa, which means that each is enabled to improve its own services and standards through its own efforts. Staying power, self-respect and independence remain intact, and when results are positive there is a genuine sense of achievement.

Assistance is only given when asked for, thus no paternalism is involved, only professionalism, and willingness to share on a business basis.

I believe implicitly that there is no future in making other countries' railways dependent on SATS. As our neighbours develop ever more efficient transport systems they will inevitably become economically stronger because of the increased trade that will be stimulated throughout the region. This will lead to a multiplier effect which will keep on creating a bigger demand for goods and transport that will be to the benefit of everyone involved.

So the wheels of prosperity will be set spinning, gaining so much momentum they will never slow down, or stop, again.

Goods train crossing the White Umfolozi River bridge — 533 metres long

Passenger train hauled by steam locomotive — one of 448 still in service (of world-wide interest)

Container cranes

*Southern Africa railway lines
network*

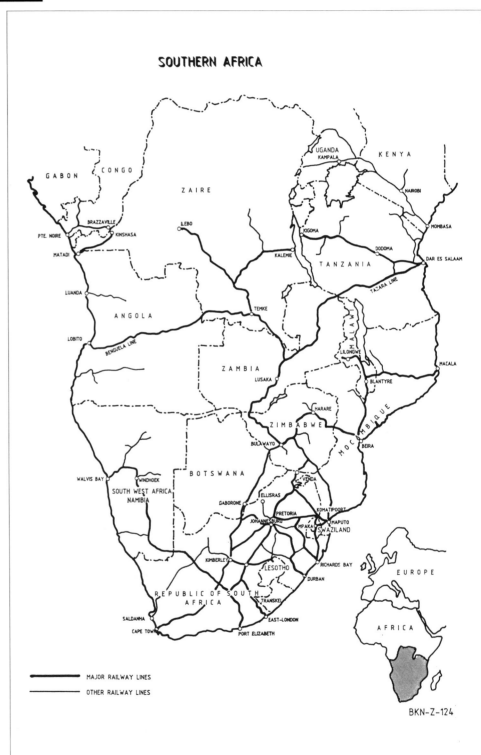

118

TREK PETROLEUM –
its strong southern Africa base gears it for a great future

SAREL J. STEYN
Chairman & Managing Director
Trek Petroleum

TREK
took its emblem
from the Zebra . . .

Black stripes – vitality
White stripes – energy
The Zebra – success

Trek, founded in 1968, is 21 years old!
The company was established to provide an important service to the South African petroleum consumer and to stimulate the economy. It has progressed remarkably and comes of age not only as a nationwide organisation but as a formidable competitor in the petroleum industry.

Selected by the Business Times section of the Sunday Times as a member of the top 100 companies on the Johannesburg Stock Exchange every year since 1974 Trek continues to go from strength to strength.

I have complete faith in South Africa and all its peoples, and firmly believe that given a fair chance we can together overcome the obstacles that confront us.

We need people who are prepared to participate wholeheartedly in the country's development, to play their part in increasing productivity, and to accept that despite our differences the responsibility of all of us is towards our country, its progress and the well-being of all its people.

It is easy to criticise, and uninformed criticism invariably becomes counter productive, especially if it contains no constructive workable solutions. It is also dangerous to criticise without informing oneself properly of the circumstances surrounding the situation being criticised.

TREK – *spirit of the African veld*

122

Trek's success is due largely to its positive attitude. Our Trek team does not have problems – only hurdles to overcome. Trek's road has no downhill side – just uphill all the time. All members of the Trek team are totally committed and have confidence in themselves and in our future.

Fortunate indeed is a company which ensures its customers are served with dedication, that provides quality products specially tailored for our conditions and developed to meet the needs of its customers. In achieving this Trek knows it is making a valuable contribution to the development of a stable economy – from which all our people will benefit.

Trek – Keeping the wheels turning

Fuel's energy — food for the subcontinent

The Group employs people of all races, and is committed to developing this key resource to meet the future needs of its subsidiary companies, the character of the communities in which they operate, and the welfare of the employees themselves.

Its manpower management policy is based upon equal opportunity for all, competitive conditions of service, and just reward in an efficient operating environment.

S·M·A·L·L B·U·S·I·N·E·S·S

CREATING JOBS
AND
NEW WEALTH

ROLE OF THE SMALL BUSINESS DEVELOPMENT CORPORATION

An important component of all successful economies is a vigorous, expanding small business sector. The virtues of small business are many and well recognised. First, small businesses utilize small amounts of capital under testing competitive conditions and thereby contribute to the efficient use of an economy's resources. Secondly, small business provides the practical means for ordinary people to exercise their economic freedom by testing their enterprise and effort in the market place where profit is the reward and measure of success. Thirdly, small business is the primary creator of new employment, and offers real prospects of self-sufficiency for large numbers of people. Fourthly, small business is innovative and flexible in its responses to market opportunities.

Dr W B VOSLOO
Managing Director
Small Business Development Corporation

127

> 'Small businesses contribute to the achievement of self-sufficiency and human dignity.'

These virtues are of special significance for the economy of southern Africa. This is an economy of abundant resources, human and natural; it has a sound infrastructure and a developed industrial and commercial sector which has the capacity to develop the rich potential of the economy. But the economy also has many of the problems associated with developing countries. Massive population growth, the concentration of this expanding population in the cities and rampant unemployment with all its attendant social problems.

In southern Africa, small business development plays a pivotal role in meeting the diverse needs of the economy and provides solutions to pressing social problems. First, small business is *the* way for large numbers of economically active people to enter the market, become economically productive and self-supporting. Secondly, small business is an adaptable form. It enhances economic activity across sectors of the economy. It allows the person with very little capital and rudimentary skills to enter the informal sector as a trader or manufacturer. Small business is also the form that may be utilized for highly innovative interventions at the cutting edge of the developed sector of the economy. The vitality of both these sectors is essential for balanced economic growth. Lastly, small business recognises the importance of economic freedom and seeks to give practical force to self-sufficiency with all the inestimable social benefits this brings.

The Small Business Development Corporation (SBDC) was established in 1981 as a joint undertaking by the public and private sectors to promote small business in the South African economy. Although the benefits of small business are well recognised, it takes a specialist agency to realise these benefits because small businesses face a variety of obstacles: a lack of access to capital, vested interests in the economy, an excess of regulation and a need for specialist advice.

The SBDC has defined four key areas to meet the needs of small business.

> . . . small business development plays a pivotal role . . .

128

Jim Makinana started his muti shop in the back yard of his home in Langa and now successfully operates from a SBDC shopping centre

Randall Wicomb, a well-known singer, achieved business success as a coppersmith with SBDC advice and finance

Small businesses require access to capital, affordable business premises, advisory services and a body to promote the wider interests of small business. The SBDC has made considerable headway in meeting these needs. First, the SBDC offers an imaginative range of financial packages and we have been successful in meeting the financial requirements of very different kinds of business from the small trader or manufacturer in the informal sector to the more established business in the formal sector. The SBDC has granted direct loans totalling R519 million to 21 055 entrepreneurs. We have created and maintained nearly 200 000 jobs at an average cost per job opportunity of R2,382.

Secondly, the SBDC is today the leading developer of industrial and commercial business premises in black areas. We have pioneered these developments in communities long neglected as a result of past legal restriction.

Thirdly, the SBDC devotes considerable resources to advisory and training services. The SBDC handles a large volume of enquiries, currently running at 20 000 per month.

Small businesses are useful instruments in bringing development to lesser developed areas and communities; they promote greater awareness of the benefits of the free enterprise system.

Research conducted in high-growth economies reveals that small business is by far the most effective job creator in the free enterprise economy.

Port Elizabeth interior decorator Margaret Shipalana opened her shop "Bongani Home Decorators" with help from the SBDC in 1986. She was subsequently a runner-up in the Institute of Marketing Management's Emergent Entrepreneur competition and now does regular business in Transkei and Ciskei.

With the assistance of the SBDC the third world finds a place in the first world's sun

Finally, small businesses lack the time and resources to promote the wider interests of small business. The SBDC has had the institutional strength to go in to bat for small business. One area of particular importance is deregulation. The SBDC has made notable advances in this area, for example, the SBDC has helped persuade local authorities to relax the stringency of their regulations governing street vendors who are now a familiar sight on the streets of our large cities.

The SBDC is thus a successful southern African initiative, working for the well-being of all people by making small business work.

F·I·N·A·N·C·I·N·G
I·N·F·R·A·S·T·R·U·C·T·U·R·E

BANKING

EXPORTING

INSURANCE

> *"Capital,
> enterprise and courage
> are the mainsprings of progress."*

So said that man of vision, Sir Ernest Oppenheimer, Chairman of Anglo-American Corporation from 1917 to 1957, and first chairman of UAL Merchant Bank (then Union Acceptances).

G.F. RICHARDSON
Chief Executive
UAL Merchant Bank

133

The bank was formed in 1955 to be the catalyst in the creation of a short-term money market in South Africa in order to reduce the country's traditional dependence on London. Sir Ernest's vision was vindicated, and UAL, with flexibility and resourcefulness, has played a major role in the growth of the money and capital markets in South Africa.

The mobilisation of financial resources has been the springboard for accelerated development of the southern African subcontinent. Mineral exploration, agriculture, manufacturing and agro-industries, mineral processing and distribution – all were set for development.

Inevitably the power resources of the region would become severely tested, and in 1969 the great R352 million Cahora Bassa scheme was launched by the Zambian Anglo-American consortium and the South African and Portuguese governments for the construction of a 4 000 kw hydro-electric power plant harnessing the great Zambezi river in Mocambique.

For a project of this size availability of finance was a vital element. To UAL and the Banque de Paris et des Pay Bas fell the negotiating role, involving multi-national credit arrangements, pre-completion finance from South African sources, and the construction of the overall financial package. Part of UAL's role covered the negotiation of South African export credit under the then newly-created South African Export Credit scheme, with which UAL has been closely associated since.

UAL was similarly involved in the financing of the BCL copper and nickel mine at Selibe-Pikwe in Botswana in the early 1970s – a venture which was to provide Botswana's major exports before these were overtaken by diamond production.

Cahora Bassa at the time was seen to have implications far beyond the mere generation and distribution of power; its promoters saw the scheme as a catalyst for regional economic co-operation and the growing interdependence of southern African states.

That vision is no less relevant today. The future of all the states of this subcontinent must be involved in the harnessing and maximisation of the resources of the whole region.

The Lesotho Highlands Water Project is but one example. Based on the premise that Lesotho has a valuable commodity in the form of water which it could make available to South Africa at a lower cost than would be available downstream, the benefits to all became apparent. Lesotho, besides the sale of its water, gains a hydro-electric generating plant, many new roads and, critically, employment opportunities.

South Africa is ensured of water supplies into the 21st century, enabling it to continue to be the catalyst for growth in the subcontinent. The cost – some R4 billion at today's prices. This will be met by both external and internal sources, as with Cahora Bassa. Financing the project's tunnels in South Africa is being channeled through the Trans Caledonian Tunnel Authority, UAL being a member of the financing consortium.

The South African export finance scheme, more refined today than in the 1960s and 1970s, will undoubtedly play a significant role, and so UAL will continue to oil the financial wheels of that engine of growth – the economy of the southern African subcontinent.

Never was Sir Ernest's maxim as true as it is today.

Cahora Bassa

The Lesotho Highlands water project enables Lesotho to sell water to South Africa and as a result gain a hydro-electric generating plant, many new roads, and employment opportunities

136

SOUTH AFRICA AND AFRICA
economic realism in the decade ahead

During the past decade significant shifts have taken place in the northern hemisphere towards greater economic realism. These developments are now affecting Africa and may determine our future in the southern region of the continent during the last decade of the century.

Economic issues have become more central to our thinking as political rhetoric, social engineering and ideology have proved to be cul-de-sacs. Economic growth, prosperity through market principles and commercial realism have become priority issues.

In southern Africa the Namibia/Angola initiative has been the trigger mechanism that has given greater meaning to the outward economic moves into southern Africa that have taken place in the business sector during the last decade.

Africa seems to become more central in our thinking not only in the political corridors and the echelons of business power, but at all possible levels throughout the community in South Africa. African states realise that the honeymoon of massive foreign aid without strings is coming to an end. Recipient countries will have to demonstrate great-

W.B. HOLTES
Chief Executive
SAFTO

137

er economic realism. International loans and technical aid will become less available to those who will not be responsive to the need for greater managerial disciplines in their national economies and in their foreign relations.

The reality of South Africa as the economic locomotive will only be more readily accepted by our neighbouring countries if we are seen to be effectively pulling along the economies of our partners in southern Africa. Business is a two-way street. Long term economic relations may require a commitment to joint ventures in the infrastructure supporting the region's foreign trade development. Improved railway systems, harbours, airports and aviation, power generation, telecommunications, should all deliberately be aimed at enabling other countries in the region to become sufficiently economically successful to earn the foreign exchange needed for greater confidence by those international agencies, banks and governments that will be called on to finance their economies or at least those projects that are essential to achieve at least a modicum of economic growth.

This may all sound like far-fetched idealism. Far from it. It is enlightened self-interest for South Africa to be surrounded by prosperous countries rather than by economic basket-cases. This is the economic history of the world; this is also the global economic reality abroad. Most successful economies internationally have grown on the basis of prosperous economic relations with their neighbouring states. In fact, there is no country in the world that has had such little economic interchange with its neighbours as South Africa, and as a result it has had to become a successful distant marketer, selling more than 90% of its products over huge distances of 10 000 km and more to its foreign markets.

It will take many years to achieve a gradual change in this respect. When looking back it is only 20 years ago that South Africa was utterly dependent on its trade with Britain and the Commonwealth. Today South Africa is a success story of a country having successfully diversified its foreign trade over more than a hundred foreign markets right across Europe, the Middle and Far East and the Americas. The next wave in our trade development should aim at Africa in spite of all its limitations of foreign exchange restraints and stalling economic growth patterns. It will obviously not be the massive industrial market that the bulk of our primary exports needs, but at least it will offer us an opportunity towards product diversification that has so far eluded us.

Only in Africa can we broaden our narrow primary export base to a product and services basket more in line with the total range of our economy. In fact, as the successful Africa marketers can witness, there is virtually no product or service successfully sold in South Africa that cannot be marketed in southern Africa competitively over foreign suppliers. Our current Africa trade is estimated at 10% of total exports or about R4,9 billion: most of this is in manufactured or processed products.

All these reasons are economic self-interest enough to balance the idealism of accepting that we are part of Africa and that only through Africa can South Africa find its way back into the world.

138

CREDIT INSURANCE
– covering the risk

I have been involved with credit insurance now for more than 30 years. It has meant an involvement with money, yet no money is ever advanced by the credit insurer. Credit insurance deals with the risk surrounding money, and therefore lends a distinctive perspective to the role money (or rather the use of it) plays in the creation of wealth, and to circumstances that can place it at risk.

It is important to recognise that what we here at the southern tip of Africa shared with Europe was not purely a cultural heritage but rather a first world approach to the organisation of our way of life and to our methods of creating wealth. Possibly the most important factor we inherited is the search for standards and practices (let us call them first world standards), and it is the implementation of these which will yield us the requisite quality of life through the creation of wealth.

J.J. BOUWER (B.Comm LLB)
Vice-Chairman
Credit Guarantee Insurance Corporation of Africa

It is axiomatic that if we wish to perpetuate these standards we must do everything we can to enable our neighbours to also strive for these standards. We need to give them the opportunity of being able to work together in the field of business for them to realise in real life the know-how and disciplines involved in creating wealth.

Southern Africa is our hinterland. In all spheres, technical, agricultural, health, education and perhaps most importantly business they need us and we need them.

Two-way trade is a prerequisite in any international trading relationship because the more lucrative business can be made for the business partner the more he will be willing and able to spend with the one wishing to sell to him. Secondly, African countries being generally poor their ability to purchase is limited. On top of this is the dark cloud of third world debt that hangs over our underdeveloped neighbours. This makes it difficult for them to generate, and pay for, development projects.

These states are limited too in their knowledge of marketing, and have a real need to acquire various other skills. Our businessmen are therefore well advised to do what other South Africans have already done with success, and that is to enter into joint ventureship with businessmen in our neighbouring states to integrate their own supply efforts and accompanying capabilities with manufacturing or distribution undertakings in those countries.

Important in such an approach would be to incorporate members of the communities involved into the projects so that first world skills can be passed on, not only in technically operating the projects, but also in applying business management and marketing skills so that a profit is made. Such projects are not then a drain on the countries concerned, but act as a stimulus to the still third world orientated partners.

> My vision for the future of southern Africa is one of considerable hope provided South Africa is enabled to play a positive economic role.

Africa has in its southern tip a nucleus of first world business entrepreneurs and managers who can combine their know-how with the third world sector of the subcontinent and develop the skills and resources needed to create wealth. Only if one could, through everyday practical contact and working together, develop a respect for the role of money and the dedication to make it work productively could one enlarge the first world segment (of whatever colour) of the population.

> The business perspectives and disciplines of this segment will be the only guarantee, in the long run, that we will have real growth of wealth on this subcontinent.

The need for an improved economic growth rate is possibly one of the most daunting challenges with which we are faced within southern Africa. At present it is considered to be the main factor governing aspects such as the creation of employment and the generation of wealth. Furthermore it is believed that the entire future of southern Africa hinges upon the reduction of unemployment and the creation of greater wealth per capita. This in itself should go a long way to bringing about a more productive and peaceful society within southern Africa.

NIEL KRIGE
Managing Director
Momentum Life

141

The role of the life assurance industry in the economy of southern Africa

A high growth rate, however, requires increasingly higher capital resources and it has become relatively more costly to increase the output of the economy to create new employment opportunities. Unlike other parts of the world South Africa (which is still a developing country) does not receive a capital flow from other developed economies. To be able to produce the required capital it is clear that the level of local savings and personal savings are the most significant areas that can be looked to.

Since 1982 the strong increase in government consumption has had a negative effect on this avenue whilst the corporate sector on the other hand cannot provide stable, long term finance without taxing financial resources to their maximum. The personal savings rate which averaged the 10,2% mark during the latter part of the seventies has shown a rapid decrease to approximately 2,8% during 1987. During that same year the premium income of the members of the Life Offices Association amounted to R13 558 million – more than 5 times that of the personal savings level of R2 692 million for the same year.

If a large percentage of personal savings (1982) had not been captured into a contractual form such as life assurance, total personal savings would in fact have been negative. It is particularly pension funds and life assurance policies, which are not cashable without loss or substantial notice, that are responsible for these attractive figures.

In 1987 life assurers held approximately 15% of public sector securities, 38% of domestic marketable stock of local authorities, 12% of total capitalised funds on the Johannesburg Stock Exchange as well as a number of substantial crossholdings. These investments provide the mining sector, commerce and industry with substantial capital for the creation of career opportunities and for making venture capital available where needed. Furthermore, by its investment in property, the life assurance industry creates employment opportunities within the building industry when providing the shops, factories and office accommodation required by industry and commerce.

With the severe housing shortage (in South Africa alone there is a shortfall of more than 3,5 million homes – at an estimated cost of R5 000 million) a substantial amount of capital has to be mobilised to address housing backlogs for middle to lower income communities throughout southern Africa. The life assurance industry sees its role as being more indirect here – i.e. funds are being mobilised and channelled to institutions which are specifically equipped to solve housing problems, to create job opportunities and to develop smaller informal companies.

Lastly, but most important, is the vital role that life offices play in assisting individuals in providing for their own needs, particularly after retirement. As an example I quote the total benefits paid out by life offices in 1987 which amounted to R5 3 billion in comparison to an amount of R2 21 billion budgeted for by the Department of National Health and Population Development in their 1987/1988 budget and the amount of R0 9 billion paid out in social pensions by the government in 1986.

C·I·V·I·L E·N·G·I·N·E·E·R·I·N·G

SKILLS BASE FOR
THE SUBCONTINENT'S
DEVELOPMENT

CIVIL ENGINEERING
CONTRACTORS
vital to the development of the subcontinent

A *hundred or so years ago men walked the length and breadth of Africa using man-made footpaths or wild animal game paths. Then came the oxwagon and gradually a system of unpaved roads and tracks developed to link towns and villages.*

Today thousands of kilometres of modern, surfaced roads have been built, and people can now travel by car or bus to work, can go long distances to enjoy their holidays; and of course these roads facilitate the efficient transportation of agricultural produce, manufactured goods, mineral products, etc.

K. LAGAAY
Executive Director

145

Add the vast network of railway lines that link all parts of southern Africa – the development of which largely preceded the modern road system; and complete the transportation picture by adding the harbours and airports that play such an essential role in economic development. All constructed by the civil engineering industry.

Go on to the building of dams, of reservoirs, of pipelines, of pump stations and water purification works that provide the ever-increasing population with clean, drinkable water. Public health is further served by the industry providing towns and villages and cities with sewerage and industrial effluent treatment plants.

It is difficult to imagine modern life without electricity, petrol and diesel oil – the industry plays a major role in the construction of power stations, oil installations and pipelines. And in the field of telecommunications it constructs the radio and television towers, as well as the microwave towers for the telephone system.

In addition to providing agriculture, mining, industry and commerce with transport and communications facilities and with water and electricity, it builds grain silos and coal or ore bunkers, mining headgears and reduction plants, and heavy industrial installations. It also serves the community by constructing sportsfields and recreation facilities.

A significant advantage our consulting engineers and civil engineering contractors enjoy is that we have been operating in the subcontinent for many years, and are familiar with local needs as well as conditions, with climate and with materials and other resources.

Our South African civil engineering contracting industry consists of several hundred small, medium and large companies which employ a very large number of people. Building roads, grain silos, mining installations and other works as far afield as Malawi and Zaire are but part of everyday operations. Our many engineers, and other senior staff, have first-hand experience of working throughout the subcontinent. A lessening of tensions, and closer economic cooperation, would enable the industry to make a major contribution to the expansion and maintenance of the infrastructures of the states that make up southern Africa.

The development of the resources of southern Africa and increased investment to modernise and expand agriculture, mining and industry would create new employment opportunities and raise the standard of living of the subcontinent's ever-growing population.

146

Du Toit's Kloof Tunnel

S M GOLDSTEIN

One of the 12 sludge digesters constructed by Goldstein Civil Transvaal at the eMbalenhle Sewage Works, near Secunda in the Eastern Transvaal. The R11 million project represents six phases of an eight-phase development. The sewage works, which serve a township with population 50 000, will ultimately process 14,2 mℓ sewage per day (164ℓ per second).

Sludge digester

John Ross Bridge

A world record being established. Grinaker Construction built the 412 metre long bridge with a deck weighing 7 800 tons across the Tugela River in only eighty-nine days

149

Port St. Johns road under construction

N3 section between Tugela River and Vaalkrans, a 10,8 km freeway

Rand Water Board filtration plant, Vereeniging

·H·E·L·P·I·N·G·
B·L·A·C·K B·U·S·I·N·E·S·S

A HELPING HAND
FROM
CANADIAN BUSINESSMEN

*T*he Association was formed
in 1987, and despite its short
existence has an impressive
track record.

DENYS ROQUAND
Chairman
Canadian Association for
Black Business in South Africa
(Director Southern Africa – Massey Ferguson)

CANADIAN ASSOCIATION for BLACK BUSINESS in SOUTH AFRICA

The Association's purpose is to develop Black businesses to the stage where they become wealth and job creators. To achieve this CABBSA helps Black manufacturers become suppliers of their goods to South African based Canadian companies.

The Association's board, which I chair, comprises representatives of the National African Federated Chamber of Commerce, Black businessmen, and representatives of Canadian companies operating in South Africa.

CABBSA's development programme is unique in that those it assists are not given cash advances to help them develop their enterprises. The emphasis is upon acting as facilitator, and funding training in, say, management skills.

The policy is one of holding hands and allowing a business person to help him or herself.

If we discern a need for management skills we pay for the entrepreneur's training; if the bottle-neck lies in the obtaining of finance we negotiate with the banks on his behalf. Our objective is to oil the wheels to enable the entrepreunerial wagon to move ahead smoothly.

The important thing to remember when buying from Black businesses is that they are essentially Third World, and the term is not used in a derogatory sense. What we mean is that companies purchasing from Black suppliers need to show an appreciation of their historical disadvantages. Company buyers should refrain from insisting on first world standards when dealing in a largely third world situation. They need to understand that a Black supplier may sometimes not be in a position to deliver on time due to a variety of problems peculiar to his environment. Some Black suppliers might not be able to handle large orders due to inadequate financing, and this could require the buyer to pay in advance to ensure the requisite cash flow. This is what I mean when I call for a better understanding of the Third World. One needs to be more flexible, and accommodating, without necessarily sacrificing standards and quality.

CABBSA certainly does not go along with the advocates of sanctions and disinvestment, who seem to want to go on penalising already disadvantaged Blacks.

Sanctions and disinvestment can only prolong, and exacerbate, these disadvantages. Surely the best way of reversing the damage of apartheid is for foreign companies to invest more, not less, in Black upliftment programmes.

Mr Oupa Motsepe (left) discussing with Mr Denys Roquand some of the softball equipment he manufactures

Oupa Motsepe (left) and Mini Hillrand of Black Enterprise displaying some of the softball equipment

In May 1988 Oupa Motsepe, a softball fanatic, was walking the streets of Johannesburg, unemployed, when he noticed that all softball equipment used in South Africa seemed to be imported, largely from North America. He approached CABBSA, and today Oupa has a registered company that manufactures softball equipment in both Johannesburg and Soweto. He gets support from the South African Softball Association, the Botswana Softball Association, and a number of softball clubs in Zimbabwe.

Oupa intends exporting overseas as well in due course.

Geoff Mphakati
standing behind one
of his printing
machines

*Geoff Mphakati, a printer in
Mamelodi, near Pretoria, doubled his
output six months after receiving
support from Canadian companies
subscribing to the CABBSA
programme*

159

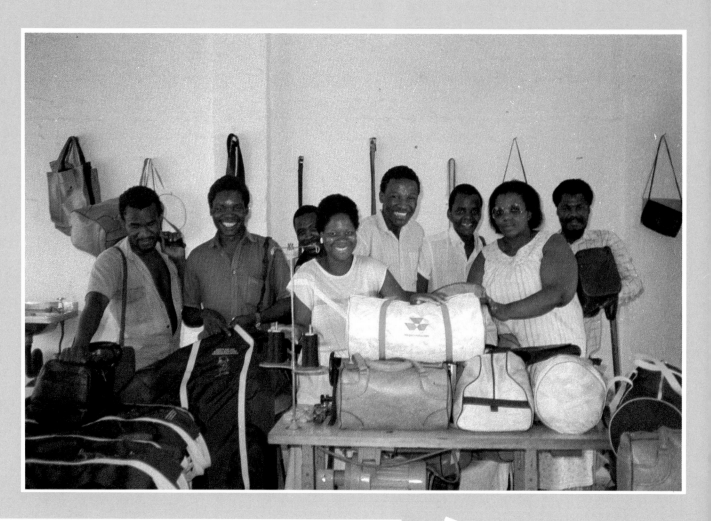

Gugulethu Kunene, a manufacturer of canvas bags in Richards Bay, quadrupled her income in less than three months after being encouraged and assisted by CABBSA, which provided her with the services of a consultant to advise on purchasing, the best ways of cutting material, and marketing. This so improved the management and technical aspects of her business that production rose significantly. Today she counts among her large customers Massey Ferguson and Richards Bay Minerals.

M·I·N·D-S·E·T

GETTING TO GRIPS
WITH TOMORROW

This world is being run by individuals who have their roots in thousands of different traditional cultures and sub-cultures. However, their influence and success, whether in business, finance, science, technology, politics, education, law or any other field of attainment, is proportionate to their adaptation to the non-traditional "culture" which comprises the international power structure that has developed and continues to maintain the System. Traditionalism and change, heritage and the future, our many traditional cultures and International Business Culture – these are the forces

Dr STUART COOK
Chief Executive
IBC

163

International Business Culture . . .

. . . is where the action is, and we in southern Africa want in on it!

which are molding or holding peoples and nations. These two forces, in constant tension with each other, may best be defined as *cultural* differences because the distinctions between them are those which are found at the very core of culture — those deeply internalized attitudes, beliefs, cognitive styles, values and assumptions which are the determining factors of our actions and motivational drives, the ''why'' behind the ''what''.

International Business Culture (IBC) is a more accurate term to describe this power structure than is "Western Culture". The West no longer has sole proprietorship of the world's business and technology. It also more accurately defines the issue than do the terms "Third World" and "First World". All people everywhere live to some degree in two worlds, one of which looks back and the other forward. Everyone has a traditional background, a heritage, but everyone at the same time also lives in a world controlled by economic and political arrangements, educational and business institutions which are part and parcel of a supra-national and supra-ethnic system which sits in the seat of power and progress. IBC is our common meeting-ground, our unity in diversity, our point of agreement.

Delegates attending seminar

Southern Africa, as perhaps no other portion of the earth, is an arena of fermentation and change. Traditional cultures are alive and strong, but no less so than is the desire and drive for more of the advantages to be gained from the products of a highly developed infrastructure.

For southern Africa this is both good news and bad news. It is good in that it brings new and fresh interest and drive into the life of our societies, a hunger for more of the advantages – or potential advantages – which IBC has to offer, an attitude of youthful enthusiasm and hope for the future. It is bad news in that the value systems and mind-sets of traditional cultures are inevitably weak or lacking in various essential characteristics which are necessary to the growth of IBC. We throughout southern Africa must grow, and not simply in material infrastructure. We have to become IBC-*minded*.

The future of southern Africa is not so much in her vast reaches of plains and mountains, farm lands and river valleys, mineral resources and oceans, as it is in her people. People make places great. They build factories and buy their output, use the roads and electricity and develop the cities. We have the "raw material" – people who would like to get along, get ahead and get going; impatient people who ambitiously want to hold a more significant position among the societies of the world. Our massive, but not impossible, task is the refining of the raw material. The secret is to isolate the characteristics – the belief-systems, ways of reasoning and attitudes – of the most successful and productive members of IBC, and then, by a structured and deliberate plan, develop in ourselves and in all of our peoples those same qualities.

Developing southern Africa into the potential powerhouse which is our dream means developing IBC-minded people. We know this is possible both by conviction and experience. Leaders, businessmen, scientists and educators are made, not born. So are farmers, mechanics and shop-keepers. It does not *necessarily* require generations to create a society which can understand, develop and maintain a complex material infrastructure. We have to make a plan to make it happen. What others before us have learned by the slow process of trial and error can be ours by a quantum-leap. For us to do so will require quantum-effort, but in view of the potential – both for success or failure – there is no acceptable alternative. Every individual on earth absorbs his or her own personal "mind-set" within a small part of one lifetime. What and how we learn can be altered, augmented and improved, if we will and if we have the way pointed out to us. Our plan is to build on the foundations of others.

166

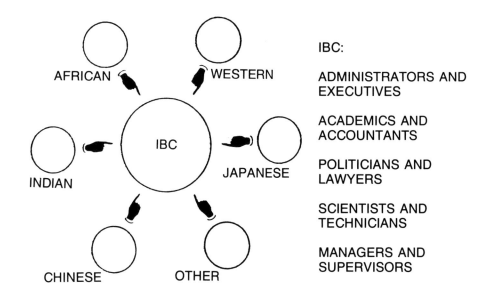

AFRICAN WESTERN

IBC

INDIAN JAPANESE

CHINESE OTHER

IBC:

ADMINISTRATORS AND
EXECUTIVES

ACADEMICS AND
ACCOUNTANTS

POLITICIANS AND
LAWYERS

SCIENTISTS AND
TECHNICIANS

MANAGERS AND
SUPERVISORS

INTERNATIONAL BUSINESS CULTURE
AND TRADITIONAL CULTURES

Traditional cultures: developed as a result of time, isolation, limited communication, ignorance of others' ways of life, adaptation to local and regional circumstances, etc. By nature they are past-oriented and tend to be resistant to change. Every individual has such a heritage which ought to be valued and appreciated, and which cannot be taken away since history cannot be altered. Yet, attempting to live exclusively within one's traditional culture limits one to the products of the past.

International Business Culture: common meeting-ground in the attitudes, belief-systems and cognitive styles which are running the world today, for better or worse. Sharing in the world which is (compared to the world which was) necessitates an IBC-mind-set, which can be learned and added to one's present knowledge.

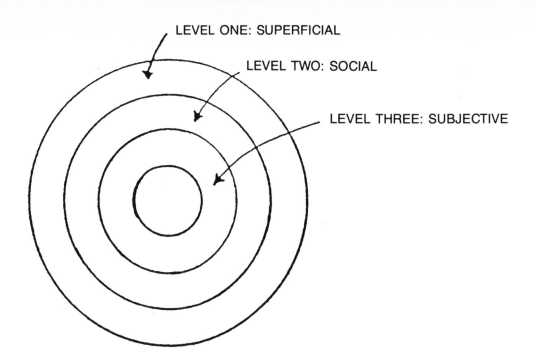

LEVEL ONE: SUPERFICIAL

LEVEL TWO: SOCIAL

LEVEL THREE: SUBJECTIVE

HOW PEOPLE CHANGE AND GROW

Superficially: adapting to material surroundings – the things which can be seen and handled – is essential to survival in each culture, traditional or IBC. Doing things with things is the relatively easy part, the province of conventional education and skills training.

Socially: Fitting into strange social settings, with the probability of new languages, manners and customs, is more difficult and psychologically more painful. Social exposure and time bridge this gap.

Subjectively: the true heart of every culture. Deeply-internalized assumptions, values and attitudes of IBC are the neglected or over-looked areas which must be bridged. This we do by means of programs specifically designed to create IBC world-views, cognitive styles, attitudes toward time, individualism, interpersonal relationships and motivational drive.

T·E·C·H·N·O·L·O·G·Y

SHAPING THE FUTURE

COMPUTERS –

CORNERSTONE OF THE FUTURE OF SOUTHERN AFRICA

FRED LUYT
Managing Director – ICL

In the subcontinent of southern Africa the last decade of this century will be a period of unprecedented development, and as yet unimagined prosperity will flow therefrom. The sub-continent has the potential to be the stage upon which the dramatic emergence of an uplifted third world as an economic force could well be enacted.

Two of ICL's locally developed products ELF and ELF 11 personal computers

Because of their South African character and the needs of the market for locally sourced products both units have proved exceedingly popular

172

There are various sources of wealth which need to be unlocked if the people of southern Africa are to access the multi-faceted economic treasures of the region. A major contributor to this potential gold mine of prosperity is the technology industry. Its development over the past three decades has been prodigious, and despite the fact that this development could be seen as a modern miracle it merely represents a foundation upon which the future well-being of the subcontinent will be built.

The rampant march of technology has, in a relatively short time, carried the world of computers through a period of evolution which now makes it possible for almost anyone to achieve whatever they wish. Twenty years ago this was constrained by the capabilities of computers. Today the only inhibiting factor is the ability of people – and thus the education of people is undoubtedly a vital application area for this developing part of the world.

Currently available technology makes it possible to apply computers to education and to training at all levels, from pre-school to university graduation. Computers will in effect become the teachers while the education planners will utilise their specialised skills to create the programs that will make this possible. Key to this philosophy is the fact that computers will have to "teach" not only computer literacy but also a limitless number of other things, including full school curricula.

This will naturally remove the mystique which to an extent still surrounds computers, and will lead inevitably to people using their own initiative in applying computers to an endless range of application areas.

"There are various sources of wealth which need to be unlocked if the people of southern Africa are to access the multi-faceted economic treasures of the region . . ."

Local skills have been developed for the exacting tasks which have to be performed in the manufacturing process

"This will naturally remove the mystique which to an extent still surrounds computers and will lead inevitably to people using their own initiative in applying computers to an endless range of application areas."

Computer network terminals are extensively used within ICL by all

ICL already sees this happening. We see the mining industry making impressive progress by using computers to analyse ore samples, which makes mining more cost effective. We see agriculture applying computers for the optimisation of area yield of crops. More and more are computers being applied to the successful running of small businesses. Air and rail systems, retail and financial services, the world of medicine, government operations – to name but a few – are consistently being improved with the aid of computers.

The myth that computers will replace people, and create unemployment, has to be laid to rest once and for all. The ingenuity of man transcends such a misguided belief. When people have been educated to a level of practical literacy, and computers have been accepted as a viable means of achieving this, a whole flood of ingenuity will go on being unleashed.

Surely this is the key to unlocking the full economic potential of the sub-continent. While politics and warfare currently strive for the upper hand in the struggle for power it will be the economic well-being of the people that will win the day.

Not only will technology play a significant role in achieving this but artificial barriers preventing the dissemination of knowledge will be broken down. International companies will have to play a major role because they ARE international, and can therefore utilise their international connections as the conduits along which improved knowledge will flow.

ICL, a major company with strong international connections, has the potential to export its products and its know-how to all the countries of the sub-continent – and out of this could well emerge a southern Africa economic community.

ICL's slogan *"WE SHOULD BE TALKING TO EACH OTHER"* was coined to serve the traditional purpose of developing successful liaison between ourselves and the marketplace. I feel it is more universally applicable to the world we are all working so hard to create for ourselves and for the generations which will follow.

Local self-reliance is ICL's watchword. Here a technician at ICL is engaged on component repair which until a few years ago had to be effected overseas

Local research and development fully support local manufacture. Here in the fully equipped R & D centre ICL not only perfects local products but also develops new and better techniques for local repair

176

Man stands at the dawn of the Age of Insight — a new era of understanding how things work and how to make them work better. Before the turn of the century at least ten times as much progress in science and technology will be experienced as during the past decade and this will play a critical role in strengthening the world's economies and improving the quality of life of people.

Dr CHRIS GARBERS
President, CSIR

One of the antennae used by
CSIR to receive information
from earth satellites

*This information is
invaluable for the planning
of resource development
such as mining and agriculture
and for studies of the
atmosphere of which weather
forecasting is an example*

Processed satellite data is sold extensively in
southern Africa

However, developing new technologies has become an
exceptionally sophisticated and cost-intensive process, and
alliances in the technological field are becoming vital. This
is especially important for the sub-Saharan regions of Africa, where economies and populations are for the most part
small and marred by a pronounced scarcity of high-level
manpower, particularly in the science and engineering
disciplines.

It is precisely in this area where the subcontinent stands to gain handsomely from the accumulated expertise acquired by CSIR and other institutions in the African environment, and their ability to translate first world knowledge into third world solutions.

In the 43 years of its existence CSIR has developed into a nationally and internationally respected research and development organization, unique to the African continent, and well equipped with modern facilities. As a national research and development organization, CSIR's mission is to promote prosperity and the quality of life of southern Africans through the power of its broadly-based capacity in science and technology. It can, at short notice, tackle the complex scientific problems associated with first world situations, as well as those typically arising in developing countries.

Raw materials, single crystals and processed devices are analysed by microbeams of ions or x-rays in this facility at CSIR

With its 4 400 scientists, engineers and support personnel CSIR fulfills its mission by means of two main thrusts:

1. its Foundation for Research Development (FRD) encourages the development of scientific manpower by means of grants and bursaries, manages unique national research facilities and furthers national and international scientific liaison and collaboration.

   In the financial year 1988/89 the FRD budget was R95,6 million; the CSIR's total budget R448 million.

2. Careful assessment of industry's research needs has resulted in CSIR selecting thirteen technology areas of critical importance to southern Africa, to which it now applies its expertise. These activities, consolidated in the Research, Development and Implementation (RDI) Group of the CSIR, are:
   - *advanced computing*
   - *building*
   - *earth, marine and atmospheric sciences*
   - *materials*
   - *production*
   - *processing and chemical manufacturing*
   - *aeronautics*
   - *energy*
   - *food*
   - *information*
   - *micro-electronics and communications*
   - *roads and transport*
   - *water*

   The RDI Group is currently involved in nearly 2 600 contracts with industry. Its objective is to be an effective partner in science and technology for both the public and private sectors.

CSIR researchers not only study the design of freeways but also the building and upkeep of smaller and even untarred roads

Making the best of various natural resources is one of the aims of CSIR in co-operating with the private and public sectors

One of southern Africa's resources is coal, mined here using the open-cast technique

CSIR HEADQUARTERS PRETORIA

In the 1985/86 financial year the CSIR was involved in funding and executing about 13% of all research and development undertaken on the African continent. Already benefiting from this work in a limited measure are 14 African countries availing themselves of CSIR assistance in fields such as housing, water purification, land use planning by means of satellite imagery, food technology, road construction and transport planning, combating atmospheric and water pollution, mining and materials technology.

The Bardenpho process is fairly simple to operate yet very effective

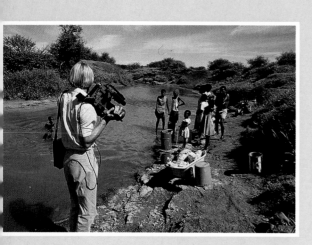

CSIR developed Bardenpho process for purifying water

Research by CSIR in rural areas where sources of water are used for drinking, washing and ablution

It is my firm belief that the CSIR is destined to play an increasingly important role in the future progress of Africa south of the Sahara, and that closer collaboration in science and technology will bring increasing wealth and peace for all who inhabit this challenging subcontinent.

P·E·R·S·O·N·A·L·I·S·E·D I·N·D·E·X

Name	Company/Organisation	Designation
Bouwer J.J.	Credit Guarantee Insurance Corporation of Africa, Ltd.	Vice-Chairman
Cook Dr. Stuart	International Business Culture	Chief Executive
Claassens G.C.D.	Department of Water Affairs	Director-General
de Romijn Lucas	Macs Maritime Carrier Shipping, Ltd.	Managing Director
Fenton Colin	Chamber of Mines of South Africa	President
Garbers Dr. Chris	Council for Scientific and Industrial Research (CSIR)	President
Givon Mrs. Linda	The Goodman Gallery	Managing Director
Harri Hans	Sanbonani Holiday Spa Shareblock, Ltd.	Managing Director
Holtes W.B.	South African Foreign Trade Organisation (SAFTO)	Chief Executive
Ireland Don	Impala Platinum, Ltd.	Managing Director
Kelly D.J.	Bates Wells – Group Services	Managing Director
Krige Niel	Momentum Life Assurance, Ltd.	Managing Director
Langley Tony	Avis Rent A Car	Managing Director
Lagaay K.	South African Federation of Civil Engineering Contractors (SAFCEC)	Executive Director
	Concor Construction, Ltd.	
	S.M. Goldstein & Co., Ltd.	
	Grinaker Construction, Ltd.	
	Basil Read, Ltd.	
	Stocks Roads, Ltd.	
	Wilson Bayly Holmes, Ltd.	
Lessing G.B.J.	S.A. Transport Services (Railways)	Chief Executive
Luyt F.J.	ICL (International Computers (SA), Ltd.)	Managing Director
McRae I.C.	Eskom	Chief Executive
Midgley Desmond C.	Specialist Consultant to WLPU Consulting Engineers	Emeritus Professor Hydraulic Engineering
Nelissen A.T.N.	Premier International, Ltd.	Chairman
Richardson Geof	Geof Richardson Associates (Architects)	Principal
Richardson G.F.	UAL Merchant Bank, Ltd.	Managing Director
Roquand Denys	Canadian Association for Black Business in South Africa	Chairman
Shaw Trevor	Zulu Nyala Game Reserve	Owner/Director
Steyn Sarel T.	Trek-Petroleum, Ltd.	Chairman and Managing Director
Szymonowicz Roman W.	Associated Automotive Distributors, Ltd.	Managing Director
Trythall I.R.	Sandoz Products, Ltd.	Head: Pharmaceutical Division
Verwoerd Dr. D.W.	Veterinary Research Institute (Onderstepoort)	Director
Vosloo Dr. W.B.	Small Business Development Corporation, Ltd.	Managing Director

Address (Postal)	Telephone	Fax	Page
Box 9244 Johannesburg 2000	(011) 886-3010	(011) 886-1027	139
Box 17175 Hillbrow 2038	(011) 642-4420	–	163
Private Bag X313 Pretoria 0001	(012) 299-9111	(012) 26-1780 or 323-4472	29
Box 2592 Johannesburg 2000	(011) 834-1416	(011) 331-3709	109
Box 61809 Marshalltown 2107	(011) 838-8211	(011) 834-1884	37
Box 395 Pretoria 0001	(012) 841-3761	(012) 86-2856	177
3b Hyde Square Hyde Park Sandton 2199	(011) 788-1113	(011) 788-9887	49
Box 1226 Parklands 2121	(011) 482-1002	(011) 726-8524	65
Box 9039 Johannesburg 2000	(011) 339-4041	(011) 339-7255	137
Box 61386 Marshalltown 2107	(011) 492-2900	(011) 836-0729	41
Box 78806 Sandton 2146	(011) 883-8800	(011) 883-5922	95
Box 7283 Pretoria 0001	(012) 322-8576	(012) 322-4090	141
Box 221 Isando 1600	(011) 974-2571	(011) 974-2683	107
Box 644 Bedfordview 2008	(011) 455-1700	(011) 455-1153	145
Box 8259 Johannesburg 2000	(011) 839-2500	(011) 837-2255	147
Box 39167 Bramley 2018	(011) 887-1700	(011) 786-5496	148
Box 75102 Garden View 2047	(011) 616-2150	(011) 616-1723	149
Box 13100 Witfield 1467	(011) 826-6631	(011) 826-1620	150
Box 39403 Bramley 2018	(011) 805-3021	(011) 805-1178	151
Box 531 Bergvlei 2012	(011) 786-5500	(011) 887-4364	152
Private Bag X47 Johannesburg 2000	(011) 773-2005	(011) 774-2665	113
Box 784612 Sandton 2146	(011) 881-5911	(011) 881-5036	171
Box 1091 Johannesburg 2000	(011) 800-3030	(011) 800-5684	15
Box 221 Rivonia 2128	(011) 803-3200	(011) 803-3222	25
Box 11100 Johannesburg 2000	(011) 446-9111	(011) 446-2207	57
Box 1781 Benoni 1500	(011) 422-1906	(011) 422-3673	3
Box 582 Johannesburg 2000	(011) 630-6111	(011) 630-6338	133
Box 2092 Northcliff 2115	(011) 888-1545	(011) 888-1349	155
Box 1775 Johannesburg 2000	(011) 23-2839	(011) 23-2319	91
Box 4448 Randburg 2125	(011) 789-2013	(011) 886-4408	119
Box 6226 Johannesburg 2000	(011) 974-2711	(011) 974-3413	101
Box 371 Randburg 2125	(011) 789-1920	(011) 886-2842	73
P.O. Onderstepoort 0110	(012) 55-4141	(012) 55-6573	82
Box 7780 Johannesburg 2000	(011) 643-7351	(011) 642-2791	127